Just Heat It 'n' Eat It!

Convenience Foods of the '40s–'60s

Adeena Sussman

PORTLAND, OREGON

Library of Congress Cataloging-in-Publication Data

Sussman, Adeena.
  Just heat it 'n' eat it! : convenience foods of the '40s - '60s / Adeena
Sussman.-- 1st American ed.
     p.   cm.
  ISBN 1-933112-19-0 (pbk. : alk. paper)
  1. Cookery. 2. Convenience foods. I. Title.
  TX714.S875 2006
  641.5--dc22

                          2005032745

Book and Cover Design: Kevin A. Welsch, Collectors Press, Inc.
Managing Editor: Lindsay Brown
Editors: Jade Chan and Jennifer Weaver-Neist
Proofreaders: Lindsay Burt and Ali McCart

Distributed by Publishers Group West

First American Edition
    ISBN 1-933112-19-0

Printed in China
9 8 7 6 5 4 3 2 1

Collectors Press books are available at special discounts for bulk purchases, premiums, and promotions. Special editions, including personalized inserts or covers, and corporate logos, can be printed in quantity for special purposes. For further information contact: Special sales, Collectors Press, Inc., P.O. Box 230986, Portland, OR 97281. Toll free: 1.800.423.1848.

For a free catalog: Toll-Free 1.800.423.1848 or visit collectorspress.com

Contents

Introduction

In the 1940s, 1950s, and 1960s, food became fun, with convenience foods helping to usher in a totally new way of cooking, eating, and entertaining. When we think about what we eat today, it's difficult to imagine making a modern meal without the help of these products. We live in an age when a hearty "homemade" breakfast probably includes pancakes made from a mix, vacuum-packed sausages encased in a airtight plastic seal, or "fresh" orange juice poured straight from the carton. Lunch might mean a few slices of cheese and meat on a roll with mayonnaise and mustard, or a microwaved bowl of ramen. Dinner could be a stir-fry seasoned with bottled teriyaki sauce; even frozen meals for the whole family wouldn't be out of the question. Today these foods are part of our nation's culinary vocabulary, with supermarkets offering aisle upon aisle of heat-it-and-eat-it options sold to help an increasingly busy population eat with relative ease. Thousands of new products are introduced every year, competing for the hearts and stomachs of a food-loving nation. But let's travel back in time to an era when the standard was homemade-or-bust and when the kitchen and its contents became part of a revolution that would forever change the way we buy, prepare, and consume food.

The post-World War II housewife was a busy woman, and advertisers were eager to lend a helping hand. Boosted by a growing economy and energized by the squeaky-clean can-do spirit of a nation at peace, it was Mom's job to manage every aspect of the household while Dad was off at work and future generations of Yuppies were at school learning how to lead America into the twenty-first century. Of course, a busy family had a big appetite; so putting three meals on the table for her brood was one of a homemaker's paramount daily duties. Needless to say, it all had to get done while making sure her hair didn't get mussed and that her apron was as spotless as the brand-new linoleum floor in the kitchen. With all that cooking, Mom certainly had her hands full, and the options were limited. Takeout was the province of the lazy, and no woman wanted to be accused of slacking off. Even though Howard Johnson's restaurants were beginning to sprout across the country, eating out was still reserved for special occasions, and the first McDonald's franchise didn't open until 1955.

Thankfully, the pantry was beginning to do its part to ensure that domestic life could be as easy-breezy as humanly possible. At the same time that Marilyn Monroe was cooing "diamonds are a girl's best friend" on the silver screen in 1953's *Gentlemen Prefer Blondes*, the pages of women's magazines were overrun with ads introducing a whole host of products destined to become a woman's real true-blue trusty companions. Forget expensive jewels—never before had such a proliferation of helpful, wacky mealtime solutions hit the market in such a short period of time, promising to ease the burden of getting breakfast, lunch, and dinner on the table in no time flat. These were the gems a woman really needed! Glistening cubes of processed meat, canned spaghetti and meatballs, glow-in-the-dark processed cheese spread, and brightly-colored gelatin formulas were trumpeted as "just like homemade" or even "better than homemade." Like the brand-new Chevrolet in the driveway, the gotta-have-it pogo stick lying in the backyard, or the shiny new Schwinn Dad brought home for the kids, convenience food was a novelty that was welcomed into the home with open arms and open mouths. Frozen, boxed, canned, powdered, or vacuum-packed, these marvels of marketing were promoted as nutritionally superior, better tasting, and fresher than Mom could make herself. Why slave over a hot stove when a can of creamed corn, a box of frozen peas, a flurry of dried onions, and a package of fish sticks could create a bona fide taste bud sensation at a reasonable cost? The American Dream machine and the food industry were like two cogs in a finely geared mechanism, and as soon as advertisers hopped on the bandwagon, the endeavor became an unstoppable train. For the woman of the house, this posed something of a dilemma. Life was busier, and it took longer to get from place to place now that families were living in the suburbs. The pressure to organize that PTA fundraiser, socialize with the ladies' auxiliary, and keep the home fires burning was a challenge. But it was still important to have dinner on the table every night by six—anything else was

positively un-American, and McCarthy-era morals only reinforced the message. In an era when conformity was considered the highest form of flattery, every woman aimed to please.

Enter the heat-it-and-eat-it revolution: The American kitchen and its contents have always been a barometer of our nation's prosperity, and things really got cooking after World War II. There seemed to be no kitchen conundrum a can of condensed mushroom soup couldn't solve, no dessert dilemma a box of Jell-O wouldn't convert into plentiful complements, no casserole dish a can of Treet luncheon meat couldn't help turn into the makings of a dinner centerpiece worthy not only of the nuclear family but of Dad's boss as well.

There was also the issue of consistency. With fresh food, there was spoilage, portion size, and availability to worry about. Opening a box, can, or vacuum-sealed package eliminated all the unnecessary worry; everything was the same, every single time. During the war years, many of our best resources were going to the troops overseas, and big food manufacturers did their part, coming up with technological and chemical innovations that made food easier to store and transport to soldiers all over the world. In fact, troops were one of the largest blocks of convenience-food eaters. Millions of K-ration meals, with their canned main course of meat or cheese (and cookies and cigarettes for dessert), were produced and consumed every night for years and helped familiarize American men with the concept of the not-totally homemade dinner. While their husbands were away, women had to make do with rationed food, stretching the barest amounts of meat, potatoes, flour, coffee, and fruit into a week's worth of meals. Ads encouraged them to eat non-rationed (read: undesirable) items, and though they obliged, they didn't like it one bit. After the war, the array of foods arriving on the scene was dizzying. Convenience foods weren't just useful; they were novel, fun, and different. As hundreds of new items hit the shelves, the possibilities seemed endless. Besides, moms had learned what it was like to spend time out of the house, as Harriet the Homemaker made way for Rosie the

Riveter. They worked in record numbers, and though women mostly returned to their traditional home-based posts after GI Joe came home, their patience for dinnertime preparation began to wear thin. Luckily, recent industrial developments, which resulted in increased practicality, extended shelf life, and portability of foods, were adapted for home consumption. Chemists took what they had learned and continued stabilizing, isolating, and enhancing every food product and artificial flavor they could get their hands on. Orange juice is one great example. At the same time the National Research Corporation found a way to dehydrate orange juice using the same methods that had worked so well on blood plasma, the U.S. government came calling with a 500,000-pound order for orange juice powder. Although the war ended and the government contract was canceled, the NRC rehydrated, then froze the liquid, effectively creating the first orange juice concentrate. Initially introduced in 1946, frozen juice in a can took the nation by storm. By 1955 more homes were serving orange juice concentrate than fresh squeezed.

While the Eureka! moments may not compare to the 1955 announcement of Jonas Salk's development of the polio vaccine, food companies saw the potential for dollar signs in positioning their wares as a boon to the busy housewife. And getting the food to them was easier than ever. Refrigerated trucks perfected by the U.S. Army morphed into the massive eighteen-wheelers whizzing billions of pounds of convenience foods from coast to coast. Manufacturers quickly caught on, realizing that in addition to their new Mixmaster, Waring blender, or pressure cooker, one of the most precious things women were clamoring for in the kitchen was extra time. To the rescue? A cupboard full of speedy recipe ideas. Three-minute gravies, fifteen-minute self-jelling pudding cakes, two-minute frostings, and five-minute dinners were bona fide kitchen stars, pulled straight from the can, box, or packet and sent almost directly to the serving platter.

With wacky convenience foods, women had the best of both worlds. Many of the products and innovations of the age were touted as money-savers as well, shaving valuable pennies off the kitchen budget. Baby food was an early participant in the convenience craze. In 1930 Dorothy Gerber, the wife of a canned food manufacturer, got fed up with cooking, hand-straining, and puréeing her young daughter's meals, and suggested that her husband attempt to automate the process at his canning facility. After several months of experiments, they hit upon a successful formula. Through advertising and the creation of the "Gerber Baby" campaign, their products were an instant sensation, telling women that they were doing their families proud, saving themselves time, and saving money. Ads promised women that powdered soup was "quick and easy." A Velveeta dinner casserole was "ready in minutes." But most important of all was that these time-saving convenience foods did not hijack the image of the American housewife lovingly tending to her flock. Delicious food had to have at least a hint of the homemade, lest people think Betty Crocker had flown the coop and was spending the weekend in Vegas with the girls. The table was still set with real dishes and flatware—their disposable counterparts weren't really part of the picture yet. Food was transferred to serving platters. And Mom was still the one carrying the food into the dining room, clearing the table, and washing the dishes—or at least loading them into her brand-new dishwasher.

Advertisers targeted their ads to the mother hen in every housewife. Cheese slices were "Kraft-protected." Canned meats were "safe from spoilage." Frozen OJ had 25 percent more vitamins than its fresh counterpart. And you never had to worry about a frozen hamburger going bad on its way from the freezer to little Jimmy's tummy—it was guaranteed to be safe and chilled in its hermetically sealed freezer package.

Suddenly convenience foods were the order of the day. To understand just how we got to the point where products like gel-encased whole canned chicken entranced the nation, we have to look at the kitchen itself. Women had come a long way from the turn of the century, when "convenience" meant anything that could be made in less than twenty-four hours over a coal or gas-fired stove. Electricity modernized the kitchen, and by the 1930s, despite the Great Depression, most American homes had a refrigerator and an electric stove. By 1937 advertisers were pushing upright freezers direct to housewives in the pages of *Life* and *McCall's*, coinciding with the proliferation of frozen foods ushered in by innovators like Clarence Birdseye. "Save on food bills! Shop only when you want to! All meals easier to prepare!" read a GE ad from the late 1930s, promising more time to devote to pursuing the good life. Kitchens were becoming more spacious and, more than before, the nerve center of the home. Building pioneers like Levitt and Sons, who built the Long Island suburb of Levittown into an icon of 1950s life, knew that in order to lure Americans to the burbs by the millions, they'd have to make the kitchen an inviting place. They made it a domestic centerpiece, outfitting it with up-to-the-minute refrigerators, dishwashers, cabinets, and a selection of the latest small appliances to hit the marketplace. Now that women had all the tools, making dinner was destined to be a breeze. And they were having a swell time shopping for convenience foods—all they had to do was visit the local supermarket, another great American invention that just celebrated its seventy-fifth anniversary. Until 1930 most food was bought from corner stores, Piggly-Wigglys, and smaller A&P stores, with additional stops at the butcher, baker, and fishmonger for essential staples. When Ralph's and King Kullen stores began to open in New York and California, they immediately changed the face of food retailing. Consumers loved the convenience of "one-stop shopping" and the chance to choose from a mind-boggling array of over one thousand products. Vendors rushed to fill the shelves, and within a decade, supermarkets had sprouted all over the country.

While getting the food was easier and the cooking environment was more pleasant, at the end of the day, Mom's workload increased along with the size of the house. One is hard-pressed to find an advertising image from the 1950s that depicts the lady of the house anywhere else but in the kitchen, with her husband's watchful eye gleaming out of the coffee pot's reflection or nodding approvingly at the piping-hot tuna-noodle casserole placed before him. Like Joanne Woodward's character in 1957's Oscar-winning *The Three Faces of Eve*, American women were suffering from multiple-personality disorder. Feminism, in the form of Betty Friedan's *The Feminine Mystique*, was still a couple of years off, but the fairer sex was beginning to bristle at the idea that nothing more than a perfectly frosted, homemade cake defined them. By 1961 women were learning to get in touch with their inner sloth and sit down for themselves, just about the time that Peg Bracken, a nonprofessional cook living in Hawaii, wrote *The Complete I Hate to Cook Cookbook*. The book didn't focus exclusively on convenience foods, but page after page was dominated by recipes with nary a fresh supermarket item in sight. Shrimp Cream Dip called for cream cheese, canned shrimp soup, Worcestershire sauce, canned olives, and curry powder. Fast Cheese Biscuits identified bread mix, grated cheddar cheese, and dried onion on the shopping list. Bracken's introduction said it all: "This book is for those of us who want to fold our big dishwater hands around a martini instead of a flounder come the end of a long day." It was a radical message, but one that found a natural ally in the convenience-foods camp.

The increasing popularity of television had a huge impact on our nation's eating habits as well. For starters, the popularity of popcorn, a food associated with the movies, slumped as more and more people sought entertainment from the smaller screen at home. Sales only rebounded with the introduction of new packaging that promised movie-fresh popcorn at home. Until the late 1940s radio was the primary form of daily entertainment and information for Americans. The most popular dramas and comedies came over the airwaves, and though they were sponsored by advertisers (the term "soap opera" was actually a byproduct of Proctor & Gamble's commercial support), they allowed listeners to imagine the environments for themselves. That all changed with the big box in the living room. Suddenly sitcoms, variety shows, and dramas gave housewives a paint-by-numbers visual picture of the ideal American kitchen, complete with brand names, style numbers, and, soon enough, color recommendations. Women could literally go to the appliance store and order the same fully outfitted, Hotpoint kitchen Harriet Nelson used as command center for feeding her hungry brood. By the 1960s shows like *Lost in Space* and *The Jetsons* helped fuel the curiosity of futurists who tried to imagine how life would be lived at the turn of the next century. Convenience foods made sense, and they were less intimidating—and far more appetizing—than the "meal in a capsule" being predicted by futurists.

Even politics got in on the easy-food act. With McCarthy on the prowl and communism perceived as a direct threat to the American way of living, people built bomb shelters in their basements, stocking them with shelf-stable foods like Bisquick and Crisco that could potentially last through a nuclear winter. As the Cold War marched on, the American meal even became a weapon in the democratic propaganda arsenal. In 1959 Richard Nixon traveled to Moscow for the famous televised "kitchen debate" against Nikita Khrushchev. As reporters and photographers followed them from display to display at the American National Exhibition in Moscow, Nixon and Khrushchev had one of their most lively exchanges in front of the model American kitchen, which was complete with gleaming American-made appliances and a pantry loaded with packaged foods stocked specifically to demonstrate the prosperity of American life. Although Khrushchev made his case for Soviet society, regular Russian citizens liked what they saw, eating and drinking their way through every morsel of food the Americans had brought with them and washing it down with thousands of gallons of free Pepsi-Cola.

Fast-forward to the present: The Soviet Union is gone, but convenience foods are more a part of our lives than ever. What began as a cottage industry blossomed into a cultural phenomenon. Unforgettable advertising icons and slogans charmed adults and children alike. New products quickly became treasured classics. And time-saving recipes comforted our enduring need for a touch of the homemade, making us feel that as much as the world was changing around us, a home-cooked meal still came at least partly from the heart.

CHAPTER 1

Just-Add Time Savers:
Boxed and One-Ingredient Foods

Born in a General Mills office in 1921, Betty Crocker's first role was to respond to the thousands of letters mailed to her parent company and supply helpful answers and yarns of folksy wisdom to baking questions vexing women across the country. Soon consumers were wondering just what Betty looked like, so she was given a face in 1936. With a crisp white blouse, perfectly coiffed brown hair, and a snappy red jacket, Betty looked like the trusted aunt or friendly neighbor, always available with a word of support or a still-warm blueberry buckle. Not too pretty and certainly not sassy, she was a dinner guest you could count on to not make waves. Betty's face began gracing bags of flour and boxes of biscuit mix, but her real coming-out occurred when she appeared on the cake mixes General Mills had concocted in the test kitchens that now bore her name. Although women loved the convenience of the cake mix—never before had putting together a fluffy, warm-from-the-oven confection been so simple—the sole act of adding water didn't bring enough of that wholesome homemade touch to desserts. It made housewives feel inadequate, as if they were serving dinner on paper plates or wearing the same dress two days in a row.

Regardless of how many time-saving innovations sprang up—Tupperware to save leftovers or the electric dishwasher—when it came down to it, moms wanted to propagate an up-to-her-elbows-in-flour image. The nice part would be to accomplish this without all that elbow grease. As usual, Betty had just the solution. Marketing General Mills—along with its counterparts at Duncan Hines—quickly reformulated the mixes to require the addition of a fresh egg to the mix, turning the cake mix into something worthy of the "homemade" moniker. It seemed that this was just the perfect solution, and cake mixes started flying off store shelves.

For every cooking quandary daily life presented, these "just-add" time savers provided the solution and required just enough work to sustain the air of effort. If Dad brought home surprise guests for dinner, Jell-O pie made the perfect dessert, ready to serve faster than Mom could say, "I made it myself!" If the kids were thirsty for a glass

of milk but *Search for Tomorrow* beckoned on the TV, Carnation could be mixed up fresh 'n' frothy in 30 seconds flat! If a lunch on the fly for the ladies had to get done lickety-split, Velveeta mac-and-cheese casserole was piping hot before "Mona Lisa" finished playing on the radio. Boxed and one-ingredient foods were truly the magic dust of Mom's modern kitchen, turning housewives into sorcerers and their stoves into modern cauldrons. With water, eggs, and oil as her basic potions, a whole range of convenience foods could be turned into a square meal with the flick of the wrist. Cakes came with their own aluminum pans and frosting packets. Bread was reconstituted in a plastic baggie, reducing Mom's dishwashing count by one more piece. No matter that homemade pancakes and fresh milk didn't really take much longer; these new foods were a treat the whole family could get behind, and they made the lady of the house feel like she was getting away with something. And to convince women that the box was mightier than the baster, advertisers soothed women with printed bromides that reassured them of their wisdom for choosing a dinner shortcut.

Now not only were these products easier for Mom but they tasted better, too. In the 1930s California's lemon growers spent big advertising dollars in magazines like *Life* and *McCall's* to promote the benefits of drinking lemonade made from fresh lemons, promoting it as the healthiest summer drink for kids. But by the 1950s they had all but given up and put their marketing muscle behind frozen lemonade, which could be enjoyed year-round, was pre-sweetened, and eliminated the need to slice, squeeze, and clean up. Nescafé promoted its instant coffee as "the modern coffee," claiming its "scientific controls" guaranteed that "gems of Nescafé" would be the best home-brewed coffee in a taste comparison every time. Before monosodium glutamate (MSG) began to garner negative PR, a 1951 ad for Dash seasoning mix made the suggestion that a blend of MSG, herbs, and garlic would enliven everything from roasts and carrot sticks to a bland marriage. "Just add" and "one simple step" added up to kitchen simplicity, and Mom was more than happy to do the math.

Look what's new from Aunt Jemima!

Buckwheats and franks—a meal in itself just 10 shakes off your shelf!

Shake up a batch of "Penny-cakes"!

You'll coin a mint of compliments when you serve Aunt Jemima tangy Buckwheat "Penny-cakes". Just slice frankfurters into "pennies" a fourth of an inch thick, and place them on hot fry-pan. Put Aunt Jemima mixings in shaker (see package directions), shake ten times, and pour over each cluster. Flip 'em once. Serve with hot syrup or barbecue sauce for a hearty lunch or supper dish. And have plenty of "seconds" ready.

The famous TWO   plus one that's NEW

Only Aunt Jemima gives you ALL THREE!

Chocolate makes it good…Baker's makes it best

This is the Instant that's delicious for drinking!

Carnation "Magic Crystals" burst into fresh flavor nonfat milk instantly—*for as little as 8¢ a quart!*

Nancy Green, a cook who worked in a judge's house in Chicago, was hired to be the face of Aunt Jemima pancakes in 1893. She later signed a lifetime contract with the Davis Milling Company to represent the brand, but was killed by a speeding car in downtown Chicago in 1923.

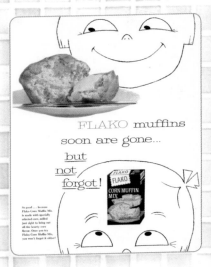

FLAKO muffins soon are gone… but not forgot!

AMAZING COFFEE DISCOVERY!

INSTANT MAXWELL HOUSE Coffee

Not a powder! Not a grind! But millions of tiny "FLAVOR BUDS" of real coffee . . . ready to burst instantly into that famous MAXWELL HOUSE FLAVOR!

Utterly unlike old-style "instants" . . . just as quick but tastes so different!

In the famous Maxwell House kitchens this superb, roaster-fresh coffee is actually brewed for you. At the very moment of perfection the water is removed by a special Maxwell House process—leaving the millions of minute "Flavor Buds".

100% Pure Coffee—No Fillers Added!

Just add hot water . . . and the bursting "Flavor Buds" flood your cup with coffee as delicious as the best you've ever brewed. One sip and you're as back to old ways!

Saves you money, too! The large economy-size jar saves up to 50¢, compared to three pounds of ground coffee!

See how the Flavor Buds "come to life" in your cup!

MAGNIFIED VIEW of new scientific "Flavor Buds" shows how exactly different they are from old-style powders and grinds.

The INSTANT you add hot water, the "Flavor Buds" burst instantly, flooding your cup with delicious coffee.

The only instant coffee with that GOOD-TO-THE-LAST-DROP flavor!

Mix date and nut breads in seconds with

Spicy Oatmeal Bread Easy-Mix

No bowls or pans to wash!

Just imagine! You mix spicy Oatmeal Bread, Date Bread, Nut Bread, and other snack breads in seconds. And you don't wash even a bowl or pan! The secret? *Every Easy-Mix package carries a throw-away mixing bag* and *baking pan.* You blend in the bag, bake in the special pan that never sticks. You get spicy Oatmeal Bread that stays moist, slices to perfection.

For variety, add nuts or fruits. Get your first package *free,* today.

Perfect Corn Bread mixed in seconds with Aunt Jemima Corn Bread Easy-Mix. No bowl or pan to wash.

Homemade Coffee Cake mixed in seconds with Aunt Jemima Coffee Cake Easy-Mix. No bowl or pan to wash.

Get a package FREE!

To tempt you to try Aunt Jemima Oatmeal Bread Easy-Mix, we offer a package free, with your purchase of other Corn Bread or Coffee Cake Easy-Mix. Just mail in the two labels, state the price you paid for the Oatmeal Bread Easy-Mix, and we'll refund you the amount. Address: Oatmeal Bread Refund Dept. 6-144, Box 6013, Chicago 80. Offer expires November 1, 1959. Please don't delay. Void where restricted, prohibited or taxed.

Aunt Jemima Easy-Mixes

No other like it!

No need to add milk to new Carnation Chocolate Drink Discovery!

amazing new all-in-one! complete, delicious with water!

ALREADY IN IT— the world's calcium and B-vitamins of fresh, whole milk!

AND FORTIFIED, TOO! with extra sunshine vitamin D, vitamins B₁, B₂ and iron!

COMPLETE, INSTANT! DELICIOUS HOT OR COLD! A wonderful hot breakfast or bedtime drink for the whole family!

FLAVOR CHILDREN LOVE! Nourishment children need—in new Carnation Magic Crystals. Just add water—bursts into chocolate-creamy goodness!

HERE'S ALL YOU DO! Simply add these wonderful new Carnation Instant Magic Crystals to water, hot or cold; stir lightly. Dissolves instantly, even in ice-cold water! So tasting, so thinking! Ready to drink—instantly!

P.S. *May be mixed with milk for double nutrition.*

Wheaties cereal sponsored the first televised commercial sports broadcast in 1939, a baseball game between the Cincinnati Reds and the Brooklyn Dodgers.

18

Good healthy drink for thirsty Ghosts and Goblins

Treat 'em with new frozen punches from Sunkist— squeezed from fresh, ripe fruit!

Party idea—*make a "Punchkin." Just hollow out a pumpkin to fit your serving bowl. Let the youngsters design the face.*

Sunkist Frozen Fruit Punches
®

Four new flavors from fresh fruit! And kids love 'em all. Real healthy, too. No artificial flavor — no artificial color.

Natural vitamin C. <u>It's the frozen punch you mix 4 to 1. Each can makes one full quart.</u> At your grocer's freezer now!

Frozen Lemonade

the new all-year fun-drink
from Sunny California

FROZEN CONCENTRATE FOR LEMONADE is as cheerful as summer sunshine...makes any gathering a party. It says to your guests that you've done something very special for them...yet is ready in seconds. All you add is water. The cost? About 3¢ a glass.

In 6 and 12 ounce no-return cans, Frozen Lemonade asks only a tiny corner of your freezing compartment. Just be sure the Frozen Lemonade you buy is packed where lemons really love to grow. Look for CALIFORNIA on every can you select from your grocer's freezer.

LEMON PRODUCTS ADVISORY BOARD, LOS ANGELES

WORLD'S BEST MIXER

Like a punch? Combine Frozen Lemonade with tea and gingerale.

Like it bubbly? Use carbonated sparkling water instead of plain.

Like it colorful? Mix it with fruit nectars, frozen or canned juices.

BRAND NAME
FRESH-
FROZEN
CONCENTRATE FOR
LEMONADE
FROM SUNNY
CALIFORNIA

Better Homes and Gardens printed its first microwave-cooking article in 1957. Today more than 80 percent of American homes have a microwave.

New! No milk to heat
just add water for luscious hot chocolate drink!

Mixes instantly! Saves your regular milk supply!

Now it's easy as pie to make

Ice Cream Pie
the "busy-day" way!

JELL-O Instant pudding • 7 FLAVORS

No freezing...
firms up in your refrigerator.
Stays creamy-smooth
and "cut-able" for hours,
thanks to
Jell-O Instant Pudding!

Which Pitcher
has the Minute Maid Orange Juice in it?

IT'S THIS ONE—with ¼ more juice for the same money than oranges squeezed at home!

These 2 Pitchers tell you better than 1000 Words why

Minute Maid *fresh-frozen* Orange Juice
is better for your health

- You get ¼ more Delicious Juice!
- You get ¼ more Healthful Vitamin C!
- You get ¼ more Body-Building Minerals...

¼ MORE FOR YOUR MONEY!

Make Yourself the Pitcher of Better Health with Minute Maid!

According to Laura Shapiro in her book *Something from the Oven: Reinventing Dinner in 1950s America,* an engineer in the 1950s successfully created a powdered formula for wine. Seems like very few were interested in drinking Chianti dust, as the product never made it to shelves.

22

$mmmm...$ **FLAPJACKS!**

Lighter, more tender! The secret is <u>Albers</u> special leavening action, a blend of choicest grains and just the right amount of real creamery buttermilk. No wonder **Albers Flapjacks** mean perfect pancakes!

FREE! FLAPJACK TURNER!

Handy 8½" for easier turning. Hardwood handle.

Simply send the words "Net Wt." from any size Albers Flapjack Mix to Albers Flapjack Turner, P. O. Box 150, Pico Rivera, Calif. Or use the handy order form you'll find at your grocer's. Void wherever taxed, prohibited or otherwise restricted by law. Offer expires Dec. 31, 1960.

◇ *another* Carnation *quality product*

Look what's new from Aunt Jemima!

Buttermilks with bananas brings 'em running!

Shakeabanana pancake breakfast!

New discovery! Sliced bananas for breakfast . . . in your pancakes! A sweet treat you can make in a shake. Just shake up Aunt Jemima Buttermilks as directed on package. Then cut a banana into thin slices and arrange in clusters of four on a well-greased griddle. Pour Aunt Jemima batter over the bananas. Bake, and serve with melted butter and syrup. And have plenty of "seconds" ready—these are sure to get calls for more!

Only Aunt Jemima gives you ALL THREE!

24

WHOOSH

REGULAR GRIND
PRESSURE PACKED
Chase & Sanborn
COFFEE

This coffee <u>tells</u> you it's fresher

It greets you with a louder *whoosh* and the livelier aroma that forecasts fresher, fuller-flavored coffee in each satisfying cup. Why? Because Chase & Sanborn Coffee is the *only* leading brand that's *pressure* packed. And

pressure packing preserves coffee freshness and flavor better than any vacuum can or bag.

Chase & Sanborn Coffees are served by more fine hotels and restaurants throughout America than any other brand.

Chase & Sanborn
Fresher because it's <u>pressure</u> packed

A remarkable new <u>instant</u> coffee is underneath this lid . . .

Yes, you can now enjoy Chase & Sanborn's famous flavor in this brand-new full-bodied instant!

THE FULL-BODIED INSTANT

New Instant Chase & Sanborn

Now—Satisfy Your
"COFFEE HUNGER"
with <u>Iced</u> NESCAFÉ®
—made in seconds with cold water!

On a sizzling summer day, there's nothing more refreshing than iced coffee. And no easier way to make delicious iced coffee than with Nescafé! Here's all you do:

Nescafé Cold Water Recipe
Dissolve one rounded teaspoonful of Nescafé in a glass half filled with cold water. Stir, add ice cubes and water to fill. Mmm, wonderful! This is iced coffee that truly *satisfies* coffee hunger!

NESCAFÉ
INSTANT
COFFEE
100% PURE COFFEE
© 1956 The Nestlé Company, Inc.

all coffee
nothing but coffee!

When you're hungry for <u>tastier</u> coffee, try Nescafé

Boxed products got a boost when Rice-A-Roni was created in 1958. After an Italian pasta manufacturer tasted his Armenian neighbor's rice pilaf, he mixed pasta and rice together with powdered chicken soup mix, and began advertising the concoction as "the San Francisco treat."

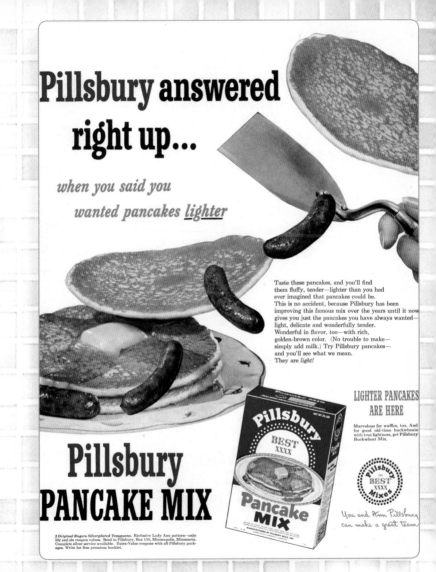

Pillsbury answered right up...

when you said you wanted pancakes lighter

Taste these pancakes, and you'll find them fluffy, tender—lighter than you had ever imagined that pancakes could be. This is no accident, because Pillsbury has been improving this famous mix over the years until it now gives you just the pancakes you have always wanted— light, delicate and wonderfully tender. Wonderful in flavor, too—with rich, golden-brown color. (No trouble to make— simply add milk.) Try Pillsbury pancakes— and you'll see what we mean. They are *light!*

LIGHTER PANCAKES ARE HERE

Marvelous for waffles, too. And for good old-time buckwheats with true lightness, get Pillsbury Buckwheat Mix.

Pillsbury
PANCAKE MIX

You and Ann Pillsbury can make a great team

2 Original Rogers Silverplated Teaspoons. Exclusive Lady Ann pattern—only 50¢ and six coupon values. Send to Pillsbury, Box 150, Minneapolis, Minnesota. Complete silver service available. Extra-Value coupons with all Pillsbury packages. Write for free premium booklet.

SPANISH RICE IN A MIX

Minute is a registered trade-mark of General Foods Corp.

Peppers, onions, seasonings—*all* in the mix. Just add tomato.

No peeling. No chopping. No work for you. The onions are sliced, peppers are diced, 9 zesty seasonings are blended with Minute Rice to make this perfect Spanish Rice . . . with wonderful old-time flavor.

So easy, so good. With this mix you can fix honest-to-goodness Spanish Rice without cooking. Just add it to canned tomatoes or tomato sauce and hot water, and let stand 20 minutes. That's all!

Thrifty meal—hearty nourishment. A package feeds 4 to 6 hungry people. Serve Minute Spanish Rice as is—or add ground beef, crumbled bacon, slivers of ham or chicken—any left-over. It's *good!*

Created for your enjoyment by General Foods Kitchens.

28

Homemade Coffee Cake
(Yes, really homemade)

Mixed in seconds…no bowl or pan to wash!

Luscious texture . . . fragrant cinnamon topping . . . and no bowl or pan to wash! The reason? *There's a throw-away Mixing Bag* *and Baking Pan* in every box of Aunt Jemima Coffee Cake Easy-Mix!

Cinnamon topping, too. Add only egg and milk, blend in the Mixing Bag and bake in the special pan. For Toasted Almond topping, Honey Butter and others, see the recipe insert.

For perfect corn bread, light, non-crumbly, *Aunt Jemima Corn Bread Easy-Mix.* Comes with mixing bag and baking pan.

For spicy oatmeal bread, fruit or nut breads, *Aunt Jemima Oatmeal Bread Easy-Mix.* Comes with mixing bag and baking pan.

Aunt Jemima Easy-Mixes

Using technology perfected during World War II, Minute Rice was introduced to consumers in 1946, cutting the cooking time of rice from one hour to 10 minutes.

This is a
CHEF BOY-AR-DEE®
Pizza.

It comes complete in one box _ including the cheese. Nothing else to buy. It's 15 minutes faster than other brands… bigger, too. One package makes one 13-inch or <u>three</u> 9-inch pizzas. It's also the most delicious.

You get all the fixings: flaky crust, tasty pizza sauce, lots of grated Italian-style cheese. (Most brands give too little or none at all.) All this for pennies a serving. Why buy anything else? Enjoy CHEF BOY-AR-DEE Pizza.

All-Birds Eye all-wonderful dinner!

You can fix it in 30 minutes flat!

Chicken of the Sea first began featuring its tow-headed mermaid on cans of tuna in 1952. Pop singer Jessica Simpson caused a stir in 2003 when she questioned the contents of the can by asking, "Is it chicken or is it fish?"

Sea and Garden Salad Dinner

All the fixin's featured at your grocer's now

Crisp, cool and hearty enough for the hungriest husband

SEA AND GARDEN SALAD DINNER

1 medium-large head of lettuce • 4 eggs, hard cooked • 3 tomatoes, peeled • 4 thick slices of your favorite cheese (Bleu, American, Swiss) • ½ cucumber sliced • 10 radishes • 1 large red or white onion, cut into rings • 2 6½ oz. cans Star-Kist Tuna, chunk style • Salad dressing

Tear lettuce into large chunks and place in salad bowl. Quarter eggs and tomatoes. Cut cheese into bite-size chunks. Add cucumber slices, radishes, onion rings. Top with Star-Kist Tuna. Toss with your favorite salad dressing. Serve chilled. Plenty for 6 hungry people.

Star-Kist Tuna

The real good meat from the sea—man-sized chunks of the prime tuna that's good enough to eat like meat

31

Now anyone can make

REAL ITALIAN

_Recipe for pizza right
on the package, too._

*Pillsbury Hot Roll Mix
    makes it easy...*

*Wilson Pork Sausage makes it
        Pizza as Pizza should be!*

Pillsbury Hot Roll Mix
(WITH FRESH-ACTING YEAST)

so good

so easy

so thrifty

PERFECT RICE IN ONLY 14 MINUTES!

What a joy to build meals around delicious *easy-does-it* River Brand or Carolina Brand Rice. Cooking time is cut to 14 minutes and you can be sure to have tender, fluffy, snowy-white rice everyone will enjoy! No compromise with flavor either! You get the natural flavor of white rice . . . just as nature intended. River Brand and Carolina Brand are budget stretchers, too. Give you up to 3 times as much rice per package as artificially processed brands. Buy 'em . . . try 'em . . . you'll never be without 'em!

14 MINUTES FROM START TO FINISH
Amazing new fast cooking recipe on every package.

RIVER BRAND
the popular low-cost regular grain rice.

CAROLINA BRAND
The King Size *extra long grain rice.*

RIVER BRAND RICE MILLS, INC.
New York, N.Y. • Houston, Texas • Memphis, Tenn. • El Campo, Texas • Eunice, La. • Jonesboro, Ark.

"STAR-KIST IS THE BEST TUNA!"

says *John Wayne*

Starring in "JET PILOT"
An RKO-Radio Technicolor Production

Sportsman John Wayne says,"Big fish are great for tall stories, but for good eating, give me the smaller tuna every time!" Only the smaller, naturally better-tasting tuna are packed under the Star-Kist label.

Try John Wayne's Favorite Star-Kist Tuna Recipe
(Serves 4 — 15¢ per serving)

Quick Recipe

Star-Kist Tuna-Kraft Dinner
1 No. ½ can Star-Kist Chunk Style Tuna
1 package Kraft Dinner
½ cup milk
3 tablespoons butter or margarine

Cook the macaroni as directed on the package. Meanwhile heat the tuna with the milk. Add the tuna and milk to the well-drained macaroni. Add the butter or margarine and the cheese from the Kraft Dinner. Blend well and serve at once.

"RECIPES OF THE STARS"
Handy, file-size packet. Favorite recipes of famous stage, screen, and radio stars! Sent FREE on request. Write: Star-Kist Tuna, Terminal Island, Calif., Dept. WL.

Star-Kist, The Tuna of the Stars"
Use it in all *your* favorite recipes too. You'll get extra flavor, extra quality, extra eye-appeal.

In 1896 a restaurant owner named Joe Marzetti began serving salad dressings at his Ohio restaurant. He eventually bottled the dressings and sold them to restaurants across the country.

"This way the noodles don't escape."

Slippery fellows, these tiny, tender enriched egg noodles.

You find them by the hundreds in Lipton Chicken Noodle Soup . . . drenched in golden chicken broth. Looks and tastes *delicious*.

Should be. It's the soup that tastes like Mother just cooked it. All Lipton Soups taste that way.

POTATO · BEEF NOODLE · ALPHABET VEGETABLE
CHICKEN RICE · TOMATO VEGETABLE · GREEN
PEA · CHICKEN NOODLE WITH MEAT · ONION
CREAM STYLE CHICKEN ; MUSHROOM · TOMATO

Lipton
Chicken Noodle Soup Mix

No other rice is this __this__ easy!

No washing!
No rinsing!
No draining!
No steaming!

Minute Rice is already cooked –
just add to boiling water and remove from heat!

Yes, Minute Rice is *really* easy! You don't have to wash, boil, drain or steam it. You just add it to boiling water, cover, take it off the burner and let it stand a few minutes!

Another favorite from General Foods

With Minute Rice there's never any danger of gummy failure. Because it's already cooked, Minute Rice gives you light, fluffy, perfect rice every time. A delicious way to balance a meal.

SURPRISE!

Buttercup Biscuits for brunch in the spring — ready in minutes!

RECIPE for a new taste adventure: your own best biscuits, baked with pink and spicy Underwood Deviled Ham and Velveeta Cheese! Just bake biscuits according to directions on package. Cover generously with flavor-making Underwood Deviled Ham... one 4½ oz. can (or two 2¼ oz. cans) to 8 biscuits. Top with tiny, plump wedges of Velveeta Cheese. Return to oven 3 minutes. Can you wait to taste that whole-ham flavor? Serve piping hot... enjoy a new flavor that blooms in the spring!

HOW TO SERVE. Team Buttercup Biscuits with a green salad for lunch. Serve them with coffee for brunch or a snack ... or at a buffet (no butter needed).

THE SECRET OF WHOLE-HAM FLAVOR

Underwood is made from whole hams, chosen for quality, perfectly cured, and blended with a secret formula of spices. Result: all the goodness of whole hams ... plus a delicious, can't-be-copied flavor.

PIZZA CRAZE SWEEPS COUNTRY

"Make it at Home with APPIAN WAY"
New Buy-word of People from
Coast to Coast

Oakland, Calif., — FOR LUNCHEON
"APPIAN WAY Pizza Pie is a favorite with our crowd, with cheese-tangy pizza sauce over ground meat, baked in a golden brown crust. Make it in minutes, too."

Baton Rouge, La., — FOR LATE PARTY SNACKS
"We all go for Appian Way Pizza Pie for its spicy pizza sauce with sausages or shrimp ... baked piping hot so easily and quickly."

Lincoln, Neb., — FOR DINNER
"For hearty appetites it's Appian Way Pizza Pie ... heaps of hamburg, special Appian Way pizza sauce with mushrooms and grated cheese ... baked in minutes in a crispy crust."

APPIAN WAY®

THE *Original* BAKE-AT-HOME

Pizza PIE MIX

It's EASY.. Just MIX, FIX, BAKE
PIPING HOT IN MINUTES AT HOME

Everything's in one package ... the flour ... fast rising yeast ... secret recipe tasty Pizza sauce

NO KNEADING ... NO ROLLING

Add your choice of fillings to taste ... sliced cheese, hamburg, chopped meat left-overs, fish ... many others

Man-sighs Pizza Pie Lightly brown ½ cup chopped onions in 2 tbbsp. oil or butter. Add 1 small green pepper, chopped; ½ lb. hamburger or 1 cup leftover meat, dash of salt. "Scramble" together until meat is done. Spread over prepared Appian Way Pizza Pie dough ... sprinkle with ½ cup grated sharp cheese ... pour Appian Way Pizza Sauce over all. Bake 400°, 20 minutes.

GET APPIAN WAY PIZZA PIE MIX TODAY
At Good Grocers Everywhere

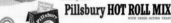

Long associated with cult leader Jim Jones, Kool-Aid was actually not the culprit in Jonestown; it was a cheap imitation called Flavor-Aid.

When introduced in 1954 by General Mills, Trix cereal contained more than 46 percent sugar.

Kool-Aid

A "Pitcher" is worth more than 10,000 words!

One 5¢ Package Makes 2 Quarts!

Your children need plenty of wholesome, thirst-quenching refreshment. Satisfy their wants quickly, easily, economically. Just call on Kool-Aid. It takes only one 5¢ package to make 10 king-size frosty, flavorful drinks . . . or 8 heaping servings of delicious, luscious frozen dessert . . . or 20 cool and colorful frozen suckers. No wonder Kool-Aid is the favorite home-made refreshment of millions.

Six Delicious Flavors

MAKES 20 FROZEN SUCKERS

KOOL-AID KID

MAKES FLAVORFUL FROZEN DESSERT —8 SERVINGS

KOOL-AID

5¢

© Perkins Products Co. 1950

"Kool-Aid" is a registered trademark of Perkins Products Co.

TASTY RECIPES ON EVERY PACKAGE—AT GROCERS

Of course you can...

Just start with a wish and some milk. Add the milk to a package of Pillsbury White Cake Mix (the luscious golden pineapple topping for each layer is baked right in the pan with the cake) and you're within minutes of a triumph. Can you do it as easy as that? Of course you can!

Delicious macaroni-and-cheese in 7 minutes cooking time

BUSY LADY ... these days *particularly* Kraft Dinner is your dish. Your main dish ... really thrifty, really fast! Just 7 minutes at the stove and Kraft Dinner gives you fluffy-light macaroni drenched in cheese goodness! The folks will love it. The cost? Only a *few cents* a serving!

4 SERVINGS IN EACH BOX

KRAFT DINNER

SMOOTH-MELTING VELVEETA GIVES YOU SWELL CHEESE SAUCE *quick!*

● Simply melt ½ pound of this famous cheese food in the top of a double boiler. Then stir in ½ cup of milk. Presto! ... satin-smooth, delicious cheese sauce is ready ... to glamorize vegetables ... to "stretch" leftover meats or fish. And ... to add fine milk nutrients as well as rich yet mild Cheddar cheese flavor!

VELVEETA

PASTEURIZED ..
DIGESTIBLE AS
MILK ITSELF

> The Kraft Macaroni & Cheese dinner was introduced in 1937 as a way to sell more macaroni noodles. By 2002 more than one million boxes were sold each day.

Worth celebrating ... Underwood Chafing Dips you make in minutes

RECIPE for one of the many festive Underwood Dips you'll be proud to serve at any party: heat together one Regular Size (2¼-oz.) can zesty Underwood Deviled Ham with ⅓ of a half-pound package Velveeta Cheese, ½ cup mayonnaise, and ½ teaspoon grated onion.

SERVE hot (but it's equally good cold), and watch your guests dip in with gusto to the new and different taste.

UNDERWOOD *Family* Size **DEVILED HAM**

WHOLE-HAM GOODNESS
Underwood is made from whole hams chosen for quality, perfectly cured, and blended with a secret formula of spices. Result: a wonderful, can't-be-copied flavor.

New Holiday Pie Idea...

Fruit Cocktail Eggnog Pie!

Start with a perfect Betty Crocker Pie Crust . . . perfectly flaky, perfectly crisp, perfectly golden brown! Betty Crocker Pie Crust Mix comes in stick form . . . rolls out easily, nestles into your pie pan in perfect shape. It's homogenized and extra-rich in shortening, too. Tastes 'specially delicious with this holiday-gay filling!

"I guarantee a perfect pie crust every time!" says *Betty Crocker*, of General Mills

THIS YEAR GIVE FOOD!

MAKE EASY FILLING WITH PREPARED EGGNOG, KNOX GELATINE, FRUIT COCKTAIL. SEE NEXT PAGE

New Holiday Pie Idea.

4 Make it light and high with Knox Gelatine

Doesn't that Fruit Cocktail Eggnog Pie recipe on the preceding page make your mouth water! What gives it that cloudlight texture and soaring height is Knox, the real, Unflavored Gelatine. Knox brings through the good natural flavors in any Gel-Cookery recipe. Use Knox for sparkling desserts, salads, main dishes.

ALL PROTEIN — NO SUGAR

The **REAL** *Gelatine*

REMEMBER: IT'S EASY AS PIE WITH PREPARED EGGNOG, KNOX GELATINE, FRUIT COCKTAIL FROM CALIFORNIA AND BETTY CROCKER PIE CRUST MIX

You need these finer spices and seasonings

to give *flavor magic* to your meals

In 1993 tests performed on a bowl of lime Jell-O with an EEG machine at a Batavia, New York, hospital confirmed that a bowl of wiggly Jell-O has brain waves identical to those of adult men and women.

LOOK! PINK PUDDIN'

New Strawberry Flavor
Jell-O Instant Pudding

JELL-O
BRAND
New
INSTANT PUDDING
No Cooking
"BUSY-DAY"
Dessert
IMITATION STRAWBERRY
FLAVOR

Good Good "BUSY-DAY" Dessert

CANNED
Fruit Cocktail
FROM CALIFORNIA

New Holiday Pie Idea...
3 Make it party-bright with fruit cocktail

Fruit cocktail's so gay to fold into the filling, to ring in a wreath round the top of your pie! And how nice for you—there's no work to do. Summery-sweet cling peaches, pears, grapes, cherries, pineapple are neatly cut, ready-fixed, happily blended in each can. Use fruit cocktail many ways these holidays, to keep your meals bright and easy!

Cling Peach Advisory Board   California Canning Pear Growers

FRUIT COCKTAIL EGGNOG PIE

1 No. 2½ can fruit cocktail
1 envelope Knox Gelatine*
1½ cups prepared eggnog
¼ teaspoon salt
1½ teaspoons vanilla
¼ teaspoon almond flavoring
1 cup whipping cream
1 9-inch baked pie shell (directions on Betty Crocker* Homogenized Pie Crust Mix package)

*Registered trade names

Drain fruit cocktail well, measure ½ cup of the syrup. Stir gelatine into syrup, set over boiling water, stir to dissolve. Remove from heat, stir into eggnog. Add salt, flavorings. Chill until mixture mounds when dropped from spoon. Whip cream. Fold into gelatine mixture with 1½ cups well drained fruit cocktail. Chill again 5 to 10 minutes, until mixture mounds. Heap into baked, cooled pie shell. Chill 2 to 4 hours. Decorate with remaining fruit before serving.

A 100-foot-high water tower shaped like a fruit cocktail can stands at the site of the former Libby's canning factory in Sunnyvale, California. The factory has been long closed, but the tower is a preserved landmark.

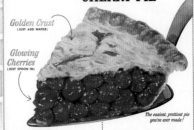

The Easy-Bake Oven was first introduced in 1963, giving little boys and girls the opportunity to bake a cake from a mix, just like mom—and with a little help from a 100-watt light bulb.

1. Hey, the dessert that's on TV!

2. Quick, while Mom's busy . . .

3. Milk . . .

4. . . . and then the puddin' stuff

5. Beat 'em up good . . .

6. Tastes swell! Boy!

7. All ready for supper

8. But I can't wait!

Fun to make—Fun to eat
the "BUSY-DAY" dessert

You can make it and serve it—
at the very last minute

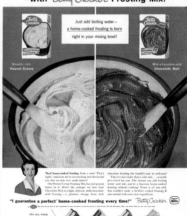

Light as a bubble !

It's fluffy-light

...no other pudding is so delightfully different! So easy to digest—never, never heavy.

It's nourishing

...the fresh eggs-and-milk dessert that's not loaded with calories.

It's so versatile

...no other pudding can change its personality so easily—with toppings, sauces, flavorings.

TODAY'S QUICK-AND-EASY
MINUTE TAPIOCA CREAM

In 1949 Theodora Smafield won $50,000 in the first Pillsbury Bake-Off for her No-Knead Water-Rising Twists, which used no convenience foods. The $1 million winning recipe in 2004, Suzanne Conrad's Oats 'n Honey Granola Pie, used a refrigerated piecrust and crushed granola bars.

Shortest recipe for real old-time Biscuit Shortcake!

JUST ADD CREAM TO BISQUICK

Bisquick makes 'em fluffy to capture lots of berry juice . . . Bisquick makes 'em rich and *short* the way an old-time shortcake has to be . . . Bisquick makes 'em easy—just add cream.

And while that shortcake's baking light and gold and good, take a look at the whole dozen baked things Bisquick helps you do. You'll never find shorter, simpler, easier-to-follow recipes anywhere than the ones Betty Crocker puts on your box of **Bisquick**

WAFFLES

BISCUITS

SHORTCAKE

PINEAPPLE UPSIDE-DOWN CAKE

VELVET-CRUMB CAKE

MEAT PIE

MUFFINS

COOKIES

DUMPLINGS

COFFEE CAKE

PANCAKES

NUT BREAD

THE 12 IN 1 MIX
Bisquick

"HOW TO MIX AND ROLL

Beautiful pie crust 4 minutes easy— with Crustquick!"

Betty Crocker

JUST ONE TENDER FLAKE and then another . . . and another. That'll be your pie crust! Might have been made by your own kitchen-wise grandma, the way it looks (*and tastes*). But *you'll* make it. And faster! With Crustquick.

4 little minutes is all it takes, to mix and roll it out. Imagine! 4 minutes! All you do with Crustquick is add water and stir it with a fork. No sifting. No guessing. No cutting in. Don't worry about over-mixing. *This* pie dough *behaves*.

And what you get . . . well! Flake on flake of delicate crust, rich and light and proud. Pumpkin pie never had it *so* good. *You* try it.

see how flaky your crust can be!

Betty Crocker Crustquick PIE CRUST MIX

General Mills, Inc.

IT'S THE

Betty Crocker pie crust mix

Betty Crocker has had her image redrawn eight times since 1936, most recently in 1996. Initially portrayed as a woman in a red jacket with grey streaks in her hair, the modern Betty has a sleek hairdo, a soft bob, and a gleaming smile.

A product of General Foods

Look! Only **one** mixing step!

* Everything goes into the bowl <u>all at once</u>.
* Beat only <u>once</u> . . . and in ⅓ less time.
* <u>Only Instant Swans Down Mixes mix in just one step</u> . . . so simple you <u>can't</u> go wrong.

* The only mix with famous Swans Down Cake Flour, so you know how good every cake will taste.

It's "Swansational"

Your Proudest Apple Pie
easier to make by far...with Apple Pyequick

Recognize this royal family of pie apples? All 4 have just the right tartness, crisp flesh that doesn't get mushy. You always get an ideal combination of choice apples in Apple Pyequick—picked at the moment of perfect ripeness.

And now look at them!—right out of the Apple Pyequick package, peeled, sliced, ready to use—*still* crisp, *still* fresh-flavored, because of a unique vacuum-drying process. Pop a slice in your mouth. Catch the natural apple flavor?

Mrs. Fred Grimm, Wautoma, Wis., has used Apple Pyequick, and says, "...have made pies for over 50 years and received many prizes ... anyone who tries your new Pyequick will find it perfect." First chance you get, try it!

Betty Crocker is a trade name of General Mills

Betty Crocker says:
"The apples come sliced, the pastry comes mixed—
Was ever a pie so easily fixed?"

YOU DON'T PEEL APPLES! What a wonderful way to make an apple pie! Simply open the Apple Pyequick package, empty the carton of crisp apple slices and spice into a bowl and add water. Almost instantly, the natural juicy freshness of these prize apples is awakened. Sweet or tart as you please—just add sugar.

YOU DON'T CUT IN SHORTENING! The other carton in your Apple Pyequick package takes care of that ticklish chore, too. It contains pie crust mix—a perfect blend of Gold Medal Enriched Flour, salt and pure, creamy all shortening—enough pastry for a full 8-inch pie. Apple Pyequick pastry can take a lot of handling, too . . . comes out tender and flaky every time.

NOW LOOK AT THE CLOCK— In less than 15 minutes, your fragrantly spiced, homemade apple pie is ready for the oven. No wonder Betty Crocker gets so many enthusiastic letters about the grand pies everyone's making with Apple Pyequick!

APPLE Pyequick
APPLE SLICES & PIECRUST MIX
Betty Crocker PRODUCT

IT'S ALWAYS APPLE PIE TIME WITH APPLE PYEQUICK

Copyright 1948, General Mills, Inc.

Ed Wood, the film director known for B-movies such as *Plan 9 from Outer Space*, got his start in 1947 as a commercial director for Pye*quick*, the "entire pie in a package" from General Mills.

After being served a piping-hot biscuit on short notice in a train's dining car, a General Mills salesman went back to the kitchen to scout out the recipe. Within a few months, *Bisquick* was on the market. Shirley Temple was an early spokesperson for the new product.

MEAT PIE DUMPLINGS COFFEE CAKE

WAFFLES SHORTCAKE COOKIES

PINEAPPLE UPSIDE-DOWN CAKE BISCUITS NUT BREAD

MUFFINS VELVET-CRUMB CAKE PANCAKES

THE 12-IN-1 MIX

All 12 begin with Bisquick

the base for so many things you bake!
Betty Crocker

A Betty Crocker Festival of Foods Special

CHAPTER 2

Heat, Eat, Enjoy:
Ready-to-Eat Meals and Sides

Gerry Thomas was a man with a problem—a 270-ton problem, to be exact. A hard-charging marketing executive at Swanson corporate headquarters in Nebraska, Thomas was challenged with converting a huge surplus of turkey meat into profits for his employer. Then he had an idea. Inspired by an aluminum tray he saw on a Pan American airlines flight, Thomas pitched to his bosses the idea of the "TV dinner"—a frozen, compartmentalized repast that could be transformed from its frosty state to a piping-hot meal in a box in just about a half hour. He claimed that the popularity of entertainment like *I Love Lucy* meant Americans would jump at the opportunity to watch their favorite shows in front of the brand-new glowing box in the living room rather than sit down to a homemade dinner. The package even came complete with an illustrated screen and dials. Although TV dinners had been around in one form or another since right after the war, his bosses loved the idea for its marketing genius, and Swanson made the TV dinner its own by promoting the meals heavily and pricing them competitively at 98 cents. The first TV dinner included whipped sweet potatoes, green peas, and slices of turkey covered with gravy. The first commercial for TV dinners ran in 1953, just about the time Americans were watching the first live national broadcast of *I Love Lucy*. The rest is history; millions of TV dinners were sold the first year alone. Women loved the simplicity of meat, vegetables, and starch all wrapped up and ready to reheat, and the family loved the newfangled fun they brought to the evening meal. TV dinners were neat! Like an early Chuck Berry song or the latest Elvis hit, these foods breathed new life into a tired supper repertoire. There were reports that men wrote hate mail to Swanson, castigating the company for hijacking the American dinner ritual, but the criticism mainly fell on deaf ears. And besides, it wasn't like TV dinners were the main course every night; on extra-busy days, they helped Mom maintain her ironclad façade of cool. "I'm late," said one TV dinner ad depicting a white-gloved mom, car keys in hand, checking her watch with a knowing smile on her face. "But dinner won't be."

Dinner also began to join the "jet set," and ready-to-eat meals and sides were a great way to capitalize on Americans' burgeoning interest in other cultures. The 1950s saw the first major wave of commercial air travel in significant numbers. Families took trips to Mexico, the Caribbean, and Europe. Businessmen flew to Asia. The results of this new adventurous spirit showed up on the plate. Chun King brought out the frozen Cantonese dinner, and La Choy lined supermarket shelves with canned chow mein and crunchy noodles. Mexican enchiladas, Hawaiian chicken, and every conceivable canned Italian specialty soon followed, helping internationalize the American palate. For those Americans who hadn't yet taken their first plane ride, international specialties were an easy way for them to bring a touch of the exotic to the home table.

There were some convenience foods that were as American as they come, notably SPAM. Perhaps the best-loved and most-hated convenience food ever created, SPAM took on a life of its own almost from the moment it was introduced in 1937. Most famous as a staple food for soldiers during World War II, SPAM certainly has its fans. By 1994 over six billion cans had been sold and countless varieties had been introduced to the marketplace, including SPAM with cheese, hickory-smoked SPAM, and SPAM Musubi—a seaweed-wrapped piece of fried SPAM on a bed of rice, which is a best-seller in its native Hawaii. There are SPAM fan sites, countless recipes, and even an entire book on the history of SPAM. Not bad for some canned ham slicked in gelatin!

For every main-course potpie, spaghetti-and-meatballs, or canned ham topped with cherry jam, there was a side dish just waiting to fill in the dinner plate. Flaky biscuits straight out of a can took the work out of mixing, kneading, rising, and baking. Baked beans became a major industry, with Heinz, Campbell's, and Van Camp's duking it out for the distinction of America's favorite. And frozen vegetables were promoted as just gathered from the field, though in reality they were being plucked from the Frigidaire. Frozen side dishes had taken the food world by storm, thanks to the resolve of a man named Clarence Birdseye. Trained as a taxidermist, he already knew a thing or two about food preservation when he realized that freezing food would be a great way to preserve it. After experimenting with fish, Birdseye realized that flash-freezing would allow people to enjoy fruits and vegetables of his labor year-round. He perfected his method, but there was just one problem: getting supermarkets to display the items appealingly. An entrepreneur through and through, Birdseye hired the American Radiator Company to build display freezers designed to aggressively and attractively showcase his 32-degree edibles in style at stores. Here's to old-fashioned American ingenuity!

NOW! ITALIAN-STYLE SPAGHETTI
WITH 6 MEATBALLS

6 (yes, 6) tender beefy meatballs with our new thin-strand spaghetti. And sauce— spicy, fragrant Italian-style. Hearty eaters say, "Magnifico!"

Franco-American
NEW!
Spaghetti
with meatballs
in tomato sauce

FRANCO-AMERICAN IS A TRADEMARK OWNED
BY THE MAKERS OF CAMPBELL'S SOUPS

FRANCO-AMERICAN

At last you can bake

a better pie every time!

Fresh-Frozen by Swanson! Fresh-Baked by YOU!

Swanson

FROZEN FRUIT PIES

Franco-American distinguished itself from other canned pasta products with its catchy jingles, most famously "oh-oh, Spaghetti-O."

WHOOPEE! It's **B&M** night at our house!

You won't have to coax very hard to get *everyone* to eat these **B&M** Brick Oven Baked Beans. The delicious brown sugar sauce, spices and tender pork that they're cooked in gives these beans a flavor that no other baked beans have. All-day-long oven baking cooks these beans through and through and makes them easy to digest. Serve **B&M** Brick Oven Baked Beans with **B&M** Corn Relish — and be sure to get some raisin-rich **B&M** Brown Bread to go with them, too.

More nutritious because they're high in protein content. Easily digested because they are baked through and through.

BURNHAM & MORRILL COMPANY
Portland, Maine

B&M brick oven
BAKED BEANS
SEALED OVEN-HOT IN BOTH GLASS JARS AND TINS

Clarence Birdseye froze nearly one million pounds of fish in the 1920s before realizing that Americans might be partial to frozen vegetables.

Recipe for Bang-up Picnic Eatin'

ON THE BEACH — IN THE WOODS — AT HOME!

BIRDS EYE FROSTED FOODS

Another Birds Eye sure-to-please!

1. **Super chicken!** Fed a super diet and kept quiet to produce juicy, tender meat. *Yes, ma'am!* Birds Eye Chicken is the eatingest chicken ever fried up and passed around at *any* picnic!

2. **So handy for outdoor cooking!** Birds Eye does all the work for you—the birds are cleaned to perfection, all cut up, ready to cook. *You* pop the meaty, waste-free pieces into the pan!

3. **Guaranteed!** If Birds Eye isn't the tastiest, tenderest, finest-quality frying chicken you ever sank your teeth into—your money back! *That* guarantee goes for Birds Eye Chicken Parts, too!

Recipe
for dewy-fresh Lima Bean Eatin'!

Cook big, thin-skinned *Birds Eye* Fordhook Lima Beans as directed on the package. Add a pat or two of butter; serve. What luscious flavor! What lovely color!

Birds Eye grows its Limas to taste and look that way. Washes and shells them for you. Birds Eye tops any Fordhooks you ever tasted. Try 'em today!

LIMAS

Products of General Foods

CALLING ALL GIRLS!

America needs nurses *desperately*—in the armed forces, in local hospitals, in industry.

YOU can help in this emergency—and equip yourself for a proud profession, too.

Enroll NOW as a student nurse. The Director of Nurses at any hospital will gladly supply details. See her TODAY!

BIRDS EYE FROSTED FOODS
CLEANED READY TO COOK
FRYING CHICKEN

BETTER BUY BIRDS EYE
—you just can't beat Birds Eye Quality!

BIRDS EYE FROSTED FOODS
CLEANED READY TO COOK
CHICKEN PARTS

Copyright 1902, General Foods Corp.

The Best
and nothing but
the best is labeled
Armour Star

ARMOUR STAR

SMOKED **Ham**
COOK BEFORE EATING

HAND PICKED
SUGAR CURED
TENDER SMOKED

America's
Luxury Ham

The leaner* meats go into Libby's
*Richer in protein...Bigger in value

NEW! *Libby's Spanish Rice*
The one with rice so firm and tender
...such zesty tasting sauce!

Libby's CHILI

Libby's BEEF STEW

So good to have on hand
for fixing meals *in minutes!*

A 1946 advertisement for canned foods called them "safe... even after the can is opened." While true, transferring canned food to other storage containers was later recommended to maintain food's freshness.

An easy cooking spree with
Wilson's Certified Meats

Time for wonderful meats—real protein nourishment—exciting dishes. Time for barbecues—snack parties—family get-together sandwiches. And Mom has time to enjoy them with Wilson's Certified easy-cooking meats. They're all featured at your store this week... from beautiful, boneless, fully-cooked hams to cold cuts for instant sandwiches. Dozens of other quick-fixin' foods at your store, too. Stock up now and enjoy a Hammock Holiday!

Kids' Own Cookout Only lean beef and tender pork go into these all-meat franks. That's why now are better than Wilson's Certified for protein youngsters need to grow on! Mildly seasoned.
Wilson's Certified Franks

Breeze of a Breakfast Wilson's Bacon is certified hand-trimmed and lean. A great protein-rich meat breakfast. To make the most of its hardwood-smoked flavor, sizzle bacon and eggs together!
Wilson's Certified Bacon

Speedy Snacks Handy as your cupboard shelf! Bif, all pure chopped beef, and Mor, the only pork luncheon meat with hickory-smoked flavor. No extra shopping for spur-of-the-moment snacks!
Wilson's Mor and Bif

WILSON'S CERTIFIED

WILSON'S CERTIFIED

Mor Bif
THE WILSON LABEL PROTECTS YOUR TABLE

There's no such thing as a 'plain' main course with vegetables like these!

flavor first

Del Monte VEGETABLES

**Sumptuous supper, California-style
—with 4 Fishermen Fishsticks**

THE PREMIUM BRAND

Fishsticks CALIFORNIA

FISHSTICKS

**Surprise Stew! Another easy treat
with Franco-American BEEF GRAVY**

Here's How!

According to the Pork Information Bureau, 65 percent of home cooks rely on convenience products as part of meal preparation an average of 3.4 times per week.

Look! "No-Stick" can
...ham _slips_ right out!

The finest container made for the finest hams sold...
an AMERICAN can for AMERICAN hams!

Thanks to Canco research, something wonderful has happened to whole canned ham. *Now* the ham slips right out! No prying or shaking, no trouble at all. You'll be delighted with the convenience of this unique Canco container. What's more, this advanced "No-Stick" Can is also *much easier to open.* A new type tear-strip winds smoothly, never "spirals." Let this quality container be your dependable guide to the most delicious ham you can buy—*American* hams packaged by *American* firms!

Much easier to open, too!

To be sure you get this new convenience
look for the oval on the can

American Can Company

Sunday dinner hash!

...because it's made from oven-roasted beef

Mary Kitchen makes this hash the way you would fix a special dish for Sunday dinner. Choice fresh beef is oven-roasted to a crusty brown. This roasted beef, with its savory pan juices, is blended with firm white potatoes, subtle seasonings. It's "Sunday dinner good"! *Suggestion:* fill partially baked squash halves with hash, allowing 20 min. for squash to finish baking, hash to heat.

Mary Kitchen Roast Beef Hash

Geo. A. Hormel & Co., Austin, Minn.

What's new on ham?

Jam!

Give Rath Hickory-Smoked Ham in a can a fruity glaze. It's sensational!

Imagine cherry jam mingling with that mellow hickory flavor. Or apricot jam baked in a bubbly amber crust. Or orange marmalade or peach jam drizzling down into that sweet, tender meat. Nothing to it—just spoon on this fruity glaze the last 20 minutes of baking. But be sure, very sure, you start with a real, old-time, corn-fed, hickory-smoked ham. And who else but Rath has it in a can?—lean and boneless—with the flavor, the fragrance only hickory-smoking gives. *Ordinarily, canned hams are not smoked.

Rath BLACK HAWK
HICKORY-SMOKED HAM IN A CAN

Ballard Oven Ready Biscuits

New easy-open full can!

9 minutes after you open this package you'll be serving hot biscuits like these

New improved Ballard Oven Ready Biscuits... higher than ever...lighter than any!

According to the Frozen Food Institute, the average American eats six packaged frozen meals a month.

Harry Lender's children expanded his successful New Haven, Connecticut, bakery by introducing the first frozen bagels to the market in 1962.

The work-free-est, farm-freshest spinach that ever ringed a dish -- Birds Eye Spinach!

BIRDS EYE
Chopped SPINACH

Product of General Foods

Every Bean

Extra Tasty

Tender *thru and thru*

Because of Libby's exclusive
DEEP-BROWN* cooking

Each nut-sweet bean
is surrounded by the full
cooking heat...cooked
clear to the heart.

NOW 3 STYLES
Vegetarian—with Libby's
own spicy tomato sauce.
With pork and tomato sauce.
Boston style—with pork and
molasses.

*U. S. Patent No. 2019143

Libby's
DEEP-Brown
Beans

Hear!
"MY TRUE STORY"
Mornings—Mon thru
Fri. ABC Network

The Potted Meat Museum is a
Chicago-based online collection
of canned meat products, from the
obscure to the mundane. Sweet Sue
canned whole chicken was added
to the museum archives on July 4,
1998.

It brings you the genius of Cantonese cookery in chow mein you merely heat

NEW!
The **Divider-Pak®** way

Freshness, brightness, flavor as never before . . . except in fine Cantonese restaurants.

Succulent chicken and sauce are cooked and packed by Chun King separately from the celery, bean sprouts, water chestnuts and other chow mein vegetables. No mushiness.

No sogginess. All the contrasting textures and flavors are guarded. You just combine contents of both the cans, heat and serve.

Chun King Chicken Chow Mein comes in three-to-four-serving size and two-serving size. A change-of-pace meal for your family with real glamour appeal! Enjoy it soon.

®Trademark Reg. by Chun King Sales, In.

Chun King's new Divider-Pak way has started millions of Americans to serving chow mein at home. It makes a wonderfully satisfying meal . . . yet is low in calories. Serve over crisp Chun King noodles and sprinkle with Chun King Soya Sauce. All ready in 15 minutes!

CHUN KING
The Royalty of American-Oriental Foods! ®

73

"This Italian favorite practically serves itself"

In the shade of a vineyard, three little Romans enjoy their spaghetti. Have you noticed young Americans eat Chef Boy-Ar-Dee Spaghetti and Meat Balls with similar gusto?

Though you live an ocean away from Rome... and have daisies at the door instead of a grapevine ... you can still enjoy true Italian food.

It's easy as opening a can of Chef Boy-Ar-Dee Spaghetti and Meat Balls.

Chef has done all the work for you, following his fine old Italian recipe. He sees to it that the strands of spaghetti are cooked to perfect tenderness... that the rich tomato-cheese sauce is slowly simmered and seasoned with special Italian spices ... that each and every meat ball is made with pure red beef, skillfully browned outside to keep in all the delicious juices.

You can have this tempting Italian dish piping hot in minutes—and for just 13¢ a serving. Chef Boy-Ar-Dee Spaghetti and Meat Balls comes in cans of 2 or 3 servings each.

Be sure to dish up plenty because that real Italian taste is irresistible!

real Italian-style
CHEF BOY-AR-DEE®
Spaghetti and Meat Balls

Unlike Betty Crocker and Aunt Jemima, Chef Boy-Ar-Dee was a real person, chef Hector Boiardi. An Italian immigrant to Cleveland, Boiardi's sauce at his own restaurant was so popular that he started his own company and eventually changed his name to the easy-to-pronounce Boy-Ar-Dee.

After World War II rationing ended, Underwood reassured housewives that its popular deviled ham would soon be readily available. The company's interim suggestion: "Just grin and spread it thin."

MORRELL

Here are Morrell Pride pure pork products—tender, mild and sweet—in three tasty, economical and convenient forms. Top-quality, prime meats. Flavored with natural spices. Like all Morrell meat products, they are made with care, sold with pride.

PRIDE

Morrell Pride Breakfast Sausage—pure pork links, spiced just right. For breakfasts, lunches, snacks.

Morrell Pride SNACK—the luncheon meat with that tasty pork flavor. Delicious hot or cold.

Morrell Pride Chopped Ham—coarse-ground, juicy lean-ham morsels combined with natural spices.

MEATS

JOHN MORRELL & CO. SINCE 1827
Ottumwa, Iowa · Sioux Falls, S. D. · Topeka, Kansas | Pork Beef Lamb Ham Bacon Sausage Canned Meats

From the Heart of Sun-Ripened Tomatoes
...AMERICA'S FAVORITE SOUP

THE SOUP MOST FOLKS LIKE BEST...

Tomatoes vine-ripened in the summer sunshine and bursting with vitamins and flavor — these are the tomatoes nutrition experts refer to when they say, "Tomatoes for health". And these are the tomatoes Campbell's use. They are skillfully blended and seasoned by an exclusive recipe, and cooked with all the "know-how" of half a century — to make Campbell's Tomato Soup.

Little wonder that, among all soups, this is the one most folks like best!

Perhaps for some time you haven't been able to find Campbell's Tomato Soup. But now your grocer has plenty — ready and waiting for your enjoyment. You'll want to serve it now and for many a tempting lunch and supper all winter long.

Here's good eating —
Here's good cheer —
America's favorite soup
Is HERE !

Campbell's TOMATO SOUP

LOOK FOR THE RED-AND-WHITE LABEL.

In the 1950s many convenience foods advertised themselves as Catholic-friendly and provided special meat-free serving suggestions for Lent.

Ore-Ida Tater Tots were created when the Griggs brothers were looking for ways to supplement their French-fry business. They combined leftover potato slivers, flour and seasoning, forced the mixture through die-cut holes, and sliced off the extruded mixture. They named their creation Tater Tots.

the joy of good eating

Come and get 'em . . . only Van Camp's gives you
that secret, savory tomato sauce. Heat . . . eat . . . enjoy.

Van Camp's IMPROVED **PORK** AND **BEANS** PREPARED WITH TOMATO SAUCE

Stokely's Finest

Stokely's Finest GREEN PEAS FROZEN FOODS

Golden, luscious peaches . . .
fresh-picked, fresh-packed, fresh-tasting.

HALVES YELLOW CLING **PEACHES**

Enjoy the Garry Moore Show
CBS-TV Network,
every Thursday afternoon.

Stokely-Van Camp

TWO GREAT NAMES IN FOOD *that mean* QUICK MEALS *for you*

OSCAR MAYER'S GREAT NEW
"SACK O' SAUCE IN A CAN O' MEAT"

makes quick beef or pork meals with Fresh Cooked flavor!

An amazing improvement in canned meat meals! It's Oscar Mayer's exclusive new invention, a separate Sack O' Sauce in a Can O' Meat. Keeps sauce and meat from mingling and losing their distinctive flavors.

Here is richer, fresh-cooked flavor—because only Oscar Mayer has separate Sack O' Sauce! Get Oscar Mayer Sack O' Sauce in a can of Beef, Pork, or Wieners.

Keep several cans of the Oscar Mayer Beef, Pork, and Wieners on hand for quick, delicious meals and Barbecue-burgers. Your whole family will love the richer, fresh-cooked flavor of the savory meat and the mild Barbecue Sauce. It's a can't-be-copied sauce—a delicate blend of tomato paste, sugar, celery, vinegar, Worcestershire sauce, onion, salt, and select flavorings.

Save the one-dish meal menus on this page. They're from Oscar Mayer's own modern test kitchens. Your grocer has all the ingredients for these one-dish meals. Order today at new low prices.

U.S. INSPECTED AND PASSED BY DEPARTMENT OF AGRICULTURE EST. 537

Barbecue Beef and Noodles, Macaroni, or Spaghetti—Like homemade! A delicious dish that's quick to fix—easy on your budget! No waste in this 12-oz. can! Just smother the tender morsels of extra lean, protein-rich Oscar Mayer Beef in the mild Barbecue Sauce—finest of hundreds of recipes tested. Heat and serve in a bed of noodles, macaroni, or spaghetti. Mmmm!

Barbecue Pork and Whole Kernel Corn—Put variety in your meal planning—the easy, quick, money-saving way—with nourishing Oscar Mayer Pork! Simply heat the sweet, savory pork and stir in the delicious Barbecue Sauce. Serve on whole kernel corn or scalloped, cream-style corn and watch appetites perk up!

Barbecue Wieners and Baked Beans—The tempting Barbecue Sauce in the separate sack is ready to serve over the 7 regular-size, all meat Wieners. Made only of select beef and pork. Heat with canned baked beans for a tasty, quick meal! *For party occasions get Oscar Mayer Cocktail Wieners with Sack O' Sauce.*

 FINE MEATS Oscar Mayer **SINCE 1883**

Ask for Oscar Mayer "Yellow Band" Wieners, Liver Sausage, Pork Sausage, and Sliced Bacon at the fresh meat counter!

GENERAL OFFICES, CHICAGO, ILLINOIS

On June 11, 1939, President and First Lady Franklin and Eleanor Roosevelt served Nathan's Famous Franks to the visiting king and queen of England at their Hyde Park, New York, estate.

83

The Jolly Green Giant, an icon of canned and frozen vegetables, was derived from the name for a newly developed pea that was bigger in size but had the tenderness of its tinier predecessors.

84

"There's our man"—

You can always find the jolly Green Giant ready to welcome you from the label

The biggest thing about the Green Giant is not his size. It's the feeling of confidence you get when you see his picture on a label.

That picture talks. It tells about peas that are still babies in tenderness. Tall, golden kernels of corn with summer in every mouthful. Grown with care such as no peas or corn ever had before. Then *picked and packed at the fleeting moment of perfect flavor.*

And all this just to make your mealtime life a little happier. Any wonder he's smiling?

GREEN GIANT PEAS BRAND | **NIBLETS** BRAND WHOLE KERNEL **CORN**

NIBLETS MEXICORN BRAND | **GREEN GIANT** BRAND CREAM STYLE **CORN**

Green Giant Company, headquarters, Le Sueur, Minnesota; Fine Foods of Canada, Ltd., Tecumseh, Ontario.

Contemporary holloware and flatware in stainless steel by Georg Jensen, Inc., New York.

Easy elegance...when supper stars
Coffee-glazed Spam®

Easy to serve a dressed-up meal, with our modern packaged foods! Mashed potatoes can come from a package . . . vegetables from canned goods shelf or freezer. Almost before you know it, an elegant dinner is ready. Star of the

Hormel blend of sweet juicy pork and mild tender ham.
Coffee-glazed SPAM : score SPAM, stud with cloves. Spread with glaze mixture: ½ cup brown sugar, 2 tbsp. wine vinegar, 1½ tsp. instant coffee, ⅛ tsp. dry mustard. Bake

According to World War II lore, surplus SPAM was cut into thick slices and used as playing cards by bored GIs.

During the Y2K emergency preparedness craze, dozens of Web sites listed recommended shelf-stable foods. Crisco was the undisputed champion, with its "indefinite unopened" shelf life. Hormel corned beef came in second, with a shelf life of 96 months.

outdoors or in...it's **B&M**

Whatever you're serving when you eat outdoors . . . franks, hamburgs, steaks or cold cuts, a steaming pot of **B&M** Brick Oven Baked Beans belongs on your patio table. Baked all day long in a rich brown sugar sauce with tender pieces of selected pork, these real old New England baked beans will add a *different* flavor touch to any meal you serve.

And, don't forget to have **B&M** Corn Relish on your table, too!

B&M
brick oven
BAKED BEANS

SEALED OVEN-HOT IN BOTH GLASS JARS AND TINS

Burnham & Morrill Company , Portland, Maine

Magic Meal Makers from **DERBY**

New tricks *you* can perform in no time at all!

Chili Con Tamale ...

Criss-Cross Hashburgers ...

Bermuda-Style Spaghetti ...

Pea-Pickin' Chicken ...

SAVE 25¢ on DERBY Magic Meal Makers

CLIP OUT AND MAIL TODAY

NOT REDEEMABLE IN STORES

In 1965 Hebrew National was one of the first companies to use its kosher status as a selling point for Jews and non-Jews alike. Its slogan, "We answer to a higher authority," became a national catchphrase.

Stokely's Finest NEW PACK Peas

The Pick of the Crop

ENJOY THEM TODAY

FRESH–PICKED

FRESH–PACKED

FRESH–TASTING

Stock your shelf for winter with this sweetness of summer

Look · Listen · Enjoy — Stokely-Van Camp's Little Show
Tues. and Thurs. Evenings · NBC-TV Network

Stokely's Finest   SINCE 1898   **2 GREAT NAMES IN FOOD** *that mean* **QUICK MEALS** *for you*   Van Camp's   SINCE 1861

89

All done for you !

VEG-ALL...

7 garden-fresh vegetables...
all sliced, diced, mixed and cooked
for quick and easy <u>salads</u>...
wonderful <u>casseroles</u>... tempting,
hearty <u>stews</u>... and 5-minute
old-fashioned <u>soups</u>

VEG-ALL

mixed garden
vegetables

Use This Coupon to Get Exciting New "Main Dish Ideas"

The Larsen Company, Dept. L1, Green Bay, Wisc.
Please send "Vegetable Main Dish Ideas!" I enclose 1
label from a 1-lb. can of VEG-ALL (or 10¢ in coin) for
each series checked below:

☐ Winter-Spring series (8 recipes and menus)
☐ Summer-Fall series (8 recipes and menus)

Name_____

Address_____

City_____ State_____

You get such good things in new

Dinty Moore Beef Stew

Lean beef, tender young carrots, firm white potatoes...all in a well seasoned beef-rich gravy! That's what the Hormel folks give you, in Dinty Moore Beef Stew. That's why it's America's favorite...Why don't you try this wonderful easy way to give your family a meat-and-vegetable main dish? (There's plenty of everything in the big 1½ lb. family-size can!)

Even better now—in the new "picture" can:

Dinty Moore
BEEF STEW

A HORMEL PRODUCT

GEO. A. HORMEL & CO. AUSTIN, MINN.

IT'S NEW

It's true Italian-style CHEF BOY-AR-DEE* Lasagna. It has golden egg noodles...rich tomato sauce...juicy browned beef...tangy grated cheese. Comes ready to heat and eat. It's as tasty as it looks. Thrifty, too!

Chef
BOY-AR-DEE
Lasagna
EGG NOODLES and BEEF
in sauce with cheese

FAMILY SIZE

Five full ½ pound servings cost you only about 14¢ each. And watch the kids dig in.
...CHEF BOY-AR-DEE Lasagna! (LA-SAN-YA)

The General Electric "Monitor Top" refrigerator—the first mass-produced machine of its kind—was introduced in 1927 and sold over one million units. By the 1950s, 90 percent of American homes would have refrigerators, allowing people to change the way they stored and prepared food.

Swift's
Brookfield
Pure Pork
Sausage

MADE FRESH DAILY

Super for supper! Your favorite pure pork sausage—Swift's Brookfield! ...in links or roll. All good fresh pork with real farm-spiced flavor! Made FRESH daily in local Swift kitchens, rushed to your store. It sells fast!

Swift
101st YEAR

More than 100 Swift's Premium Table-Ready Meats are made FRESH daily in local Swift Kitchens and rushed to your store.

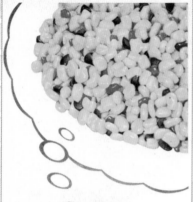

Fresh thought for tomorrow night

That's a mighty pretty picture you're dreaming up, young lady —tender young kernels of golden Niblets Brand Corn mixed with bright red and green sweet peppers. This gorgeous dish has all the summer freshness and color that special seed and our system of Flavor Farming can put into a can. "Packed at the fleeting moment of perfect flavor." Ask for Niblets Brand Mexicorn — with your old friend, the Green Giant, on the label.

Minnesota Valley Canning Company, headquarters, Le Sueur, Minnesota; Fine Foods of Canada, Ltd., Tecumseh, Ontario. Also packers of Green Giant Brand peas.

Listen to the Fred Waring Show on NBC every Friday morning for the Green Giant

Niblets Mexicorn
WHOLE KERNEL CORN WITH RED AND GREEN PEPPERS

NIBLETS MEXICORN
BRAND

"Green Giant," "Niblets" and "Mexicorn" are trademarks Reg. U. S. Pat. Off. MVCCo. © MVCCo.

"It's the only way I know to get vegetables into her..."

Your story, too! So many mothers find Campbell's Vegetable Beef Soup a lifesaver (with children who like meat but shy away from vegetables). You can expect those tender pieces of beef to disappear first. But even the hardest-to-tempt youngsters will find those six wholesome garden vegetables wonderfully good to eat, too.

Soup this good just has to be *Campbell's*

In the 1950s many companies turned the lids of their jars and cans into collectors'-item coasters. The most popular were peanut butter jar lids.

Campbell's introduced its famous Green Bean Bake in 1955. Today the company estimates that 20 million Bakes are made each week in American households.

Van Camp's DELICIOUS MEXICAN STYLE FOODS

FOR A

FIESTA

OF GOOD EATING

Van Camp's . . . Van Camp's only . . . prepares for you such a variety of exciting foods that perk up interest in any meal . . . make your parties different. Every dish temptingly seasoned . . . all rich in flavor . . . all ready to heat . . . eat . . . enjoy.

Stokely's *Finest* SINCE 1898 — **2 GREAT NAMES IN FOOD** *that mean* **QUICK MEALS** *for you* — **Van Camp's** SINCE 1861

Van Camp's
Mexican Style
BEANS
CHILI SAUCE

Van Camp's
TAMALES
WITH SAUCE

Van Camp's
SPANISH RICE

Van Camp's
CHILI
CON CARNE
WITH BEANS

Van Camp's
CHILI
CON CARNE
Without Beans

93

Favorites from General Foods ... pioneer of frozen foods

Some freeze food ...

BIRDS EYE FREEZES FLAVOR

That's why more people buy Birds Eye than any other frozen food

Watch your grocer's ads for Birds Eye's better buys—today

HORMEL HAM

Easy Eating for Easter

Easy to prepare because it's ready-cooked in the can. A 325° oven long enough to heat through brings it to piping hot perfection. Easy to serve firm, pink, even slices because no bone is there to baffle the carver's skill. And to eat! . . . a romantic poem of tender, mild, delicious meat . . . ham at its very best. Geo. A. Hormel & Co., Austin, Minn.

HORMEL GOOD FOOD

FRIED **PREM**: *5 minutes*

APPLE PANCAKES: *20 minutes*

EQUALS: *Good food, good eating*

APPLE PANCAKES! Easy. When you've made your regular batter, stir in grated apples—one cup of this to a recipe calling for 1 cup of flour. Have 'em soon—with Prem!

LIKE SWIFT'S PREMIUM HAM, PREM IS

Sugar-cured
for extra flavor

Here's a breakfast to set a person going and keep him going strong. Prem gives it the nourishment of fresh lean meat!

And Prem makes it delicious, too, for Prem is sugar-cured—sugar-cured the exclusive Swift's Premium way! No spices are added, no heavy seasonings.

Try this economical meal—with apple pancakes. Try it real soon. You'll like Prem hot! You'll like it cold, too!

SWIFT & COMPANY: PURVEYORS OF FINE FOODS

In 1991 Paul McCartney's late wife, Linda, a longtime vegetarian activist and cookbook author, introduced a popular line of frozen vegetarian meals in England. The dinners came to the United States in 1994.

Make every meal a party meal

Make every meal a triumph. Always select MONARCH Finer Foods. They have the utmost in eye and taste appeal—look so good you can't resist them, taste so good you want more.

Try MONARCH Beets, Corn, Beans and Peas and discover why we are proud to say —MONARCH Finer Foods make every meal a party meal.

All MONARCH Foods are

definitely
finer!

You will find a complete line of MONARCH Finer Foods— over 500 of them . . . . . . but only one quality, the VERY BEST

MONARCH

World's Largest Family of Nationally Distributed Finer Foods
REID MURDOCH, Division of Consolidated Grocers Corp., Chicago, Ill.

You've got a date
WITH TENDERNESS

GREEN GIANT
GREAT BIG
TENDER
SWEET PEAS

Green Giant Peas
BRAND

Your florist doesn't sell this kind of tenderness. But your grocer does. You get it in every can of Green Giant Brand peas "picked and packed at the fleeting moment of perfect flavor." How about lifting the lid on tenderness tonight!

The Swanson TV dinner tray was inducted into the Smithsonian Institute in 1986.

Swanson added a fourth compartment to its TV dinners in 1960 to make room for desserts like apple cobbler and chocolate brownies.

Now tastier—more luscious than ever!

We've made our famous Swanson TV Brand Dinners more wonderful than ever! They have all the extra touches that make good cooking *extra* good. But don't take our word for it . . . accept this Free Dinner invitation and enjoy the luscious difference for yourself.

Swanson TV. BRAND *dinners*

Swanson and TV are trademarks owned by the makers of Campbell's Soups.

"Ah" inspiring...
SPAM* 'N' LIMAS

SPAM* 'N' LIMAS
FROM THE **HORMEL** MENU FILES

Make a Spanish sauce of canned tomatoes, chopped onions, green peppers and celery leaves with a little salt, sugar, lard. Add to fresh or frozen precooked limas in casserole, partly bury 8 or 10 slices of Spam in top, garnish with pimiento squares and bake 25 minutes at 350°.

HORMEL
GOOD FOODS

COLD OR HOT
SPAM HITS THE SPOT!

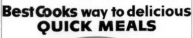

The Official SPAM fan club,
founded in 1998, has 9,000
active members. Each year 20,000
people visit the SPAM museum in its
home state of Minnesota. There was
even a $2 SPAM scratch-off lottery
ticket in 2000.

In 2003 Country Western singer Jimmy Dean was removed as spokesperson for the sausage that still bears his name. The company felt Dean was getting too old and didn't want him meddling in management decisions. Dean successfully turned around and sued the company to have his endorsement removed from its advertisements.

Pantry-Shelf Meals cost so little!

Vienna Sausage 'n' Salad Mounds! Here's supper-making made easy—on you and on that meat budget of yours, too! Shape your favorite potato salad into little individual servings—then circle the platter with mounds of Armour Star Vienna Sausages. These little smoky-flavored, skinless frankfurters are just two-bite size—and plump with selected beef and pork! Serve 'em chilled—or piping hot if you prefer. Garnish the platter with bright red radish roses.

Cheese Treets! Get credit for being an out-of-this-world cook with this heavenly meal! Treet, Armour's wonderful blend of tender pork shoulder and sugar-cured ham calls for hallelujahs every time you serve it this easy way. Place lightly fried Treet on toast buttered or margarined before toasting—add strips of Cloverbloom American Cheese. Just 3 minutes after it's put under moderate broiler heat, dinner's ready! And, remember, Treet treats your meat bill right!

Quick-Broiled Hash Slices! Men all are alike in liking Armour Star Corned Beef Hash—particularly when it's served as differently as this! Slice the contents of 2 tins into 6 thick rounds—broil 'em for 10 minutes—and then round out the meal with chili sauce and stacks of fresh green onions! It's such a good dinner—the extra-tender beef brisket has such flavor and the potatoes stay firm and white! And it's so economical—just what the budget ordered!

Tune in HINT HUNT—C B S
Monday thru Friday afternoons

The best and nothing but the best is labeled **ARMOUR**

...A quick easily served meal of New England's most famous flavor

Here's just about the best meal you've ever tasted . . . wholesome and delightfully appetizing with true, old-time "Down East" flavor. Hearty and supremely-delicious genuine New England baked beans. Beans baked for you with true, old-style, "open bean pot" goodness in famous B & M brick ovens "Down East" in Portland, Maine. Baked (not steamed) slowly for one entire day. With lots of juicy pork and spicy, "Down East" sauces. Baked till each bean is mealy and tender and an appetizing golden brown. Your first plateful will tell you how wonderfully different they are from the ordinary kind.
Burnham & Morrill Company
Portland 2, Maine.

B&M
Genuine
New England Brick-Oven
BAKED BEANS

Morton
"Old Kentucky Recipes"

demand
prize, premium fixin's

...just as you do!

THAT'S WHY
**MORTON FROZEN
HAM
DINNERS**
TASTE JUST LIKE
YOURS DO!

Thick, tender slices of hickory-smoked "Old Kentucky" ham topped with old-time raisin sauce . . . along with traditional candied sweet potatoes . . . buttered Fordhook limas . . . and wonderfully spiced, sliced apples. That's what makes Morton "Old Kentucky Recipe" Ham Dinners company-eatin'-good! Try *all seven* Morton Frozen Dinners: Ham, Beef, Salisbury Steak, Fried Chicken, Turkey, Meat Loaf, Fish. Just heat. And serve them *proudly!*

Morton
"Old Kentucky Recipe"
HAM DINNER

CHAPTER 3

From Pantry Shelf to Menu Help:
Products with Multiple Uses

It wasn't long before switch-hitting comestibles took the convenience kitchen by storm. By the time Dan Ackroyd, Gilda Radner, and Bill Murray spoofed jack-of-all-trade pantry staples in a now-famous 1976 episode of *Saturday Night Live* ("New Shimmer is a floor wax! No, it's a dessert topping!"), multiple-use food products had been around for decades. But imagine the delight of consumers back in the early days, when housewives were first let in on the secret: these low-budget recipe superheroes were capable of transforming from, say, a pancake to a biscuit to strawberry shortcake in a single bound! Just like Silly Putty, which was all the rage when it hit toy stores in 1949, the new—or at least newly marketed—packaged foods could help take dinner in a million directions in no time at all. Americans were already fascinated with convertible culture, where a car could go from ragtop to open-air pleasure vehicle with the flick of a button. While little Jimmy was playing with his Lionel train, Mom could be using the very same Starlac powdered milk she mixed into the breakfast muffins to whip up an easy chocolate cake for dessert. The advent of television was aggressively shortening the American attention span, and products had to double, triple, even quadruple duty to keep American taste-buds happy. Kool-Aid showed its many facets, proving itself to be so much more than a powdered drink. When mixed with gelatin in a lemon-lime salad, it was a shimmering vision in green. Blended with whipped topping, it became an iridescent purple sweet treat impossible to resist. Evaporated milk was whipped into sauces, cakes, and pies. And the era's competing brands of luncheon meat were positioned as barbecue-worthy and breakfast-ready—good for practically everything that could fit inside a piece of Corningware.

For a while, any ingredient that served only one function appeared to be in danger of becoming obsolete. In the 1950s Bisquick promoted its versatility by advertising itself as "a world of baking in a box." Similar to a slinky piece of lingerie hidden underneath a staid housedress, these foods were meant to make happy husbands. "Dressed to please a man," promised Ann Page salad dressings, next to a photo of an approving, bow-tied gentleman and a green salad. The message was clear: with a little help from the lady of the house, multiple-use products were kitchen concubines—subservient, flexible, and always eager to help the cause. Perhaps the biggest proponent of this genre of convenience foods was Poppy Cannon, an influential food writer and editor who penned the wildly popular *The Can-Opener Cookbook* in 1951. As food editor of *Ladies' Home Journal* at the time of the book's release, Cannon stood on one of the frilliest bully pulpits in the history of American homemaking, and she used it to encourage women to look upon the can-opener not as "a hallmark of the lazy lady and careless wife" but as a "magic wand." Her recipes elevated convenience comestibles to new heights of acceptability, discouraging women from made-from-scratch cooking and steering them towards prefab mealtime solutions.

Other authors of the era had different ideas about the role new products could play beyond the kitchen. In the early 1960s traditionalist Marabel Morgan came up with a unique way to utilize an important new invention, Saran Wrap. Introduced with great fanfare, the clingy plastic allowed a home cook to extend the life of that ambrosia surprise for a few days in the Frigidaire. As a way to keep hubby happy, Morgan encouraged women to greet their spouses at the door dressed in nothing more than a few layers of the clingy plastic. Luckily, her advice was eschewed by most smart women, who realized that transparency in a relationship could come in less compromising packages.

One great ambassador for the versatility of convenience foods that has gone the distance is the Pillsbury Company. Back in 1949 Pillsbury had the great idea to take the folksy baking contest and blow it out into a national extravaganza. The first Pillsbury Bake-Off took place at the opulent Waldorf Astoria in New York City. Women (and, surprisingly, three men) from around the country demonstrated their kitchen prowess at what was to become the best-known baking contest in the country. Theodora Smafield of Rockford, Illinois, rose to national fame, taking home $50,000 for her No-Knead Water-Rising Twists. Over the years, the contest has reflected the baking habits of American women—and Pillsbury's product line. Winning recipes often mirror the company's newest innovations and almost invariably contain at least one mainstay of the convenience-food category, from refrigerated dough to candy bars and pie crusts. This year's prize booty? $1 million, proving once and for all that convenience really does pay.

Quick, quick, quick – Smack, smack, smack!

PRE-COOKED RICE IN A PACKAGE –
sensational,
that's what it is!

★ NO WASHING!
★ NO RINSING!
★ NO DRAINING!
★ NO STEAMING!
★ PERFECT RICE
  EVERY TIME!

For perfect rice
without the work
★★★ pre-cooked

MINUTE BRAND RICE

MINUTE
RICE

NEW
PRE-COOKED

According to a Utah State University report, lasagna made from scratch cost 26 cents per serving, while frozen lasagna costs $1.14 per serving.

According to an article in *Psychology Today*, there were only a few hundred convenience foods on the market in the 1950s. In 1995, 16,863 new food products were introduced to supermarket shelves.

Wacky Uses author Joey Green recommended using Miracle Whip salad dressing as a skin exfoliator, wood furniture cleaner, hair conditioner, and sunburn salve.

Quick cooked sauces that won't lump, stiffen or separate...

...who'd ever think Best Foods Mayonnaise could be so sauce-y!

CREAMY TOMATO SAUCE! Gradually add ¼ cup milk to ½ cup Best Foods® Real Mayonnaise. Add ½ cup ketchup and 1 teaspoon lemon juice, ⅓ tsp. salt. Cook over low heat, just 3 minutes. Stir constantly. Whole-egg Best Foods makes this perfect on macaroni, rice and egg dishes, too. Serve it hot and delicious! **THIS IS THE PLACE FOR BEST FOODS**

EASY WHITE SAUCE! Gradually add ½ cup milk to ½ cup Best Foods Real Mayonnaise. Season with salt, pepper. Cook over low heat, just 3 minutes, stirring constantly. Use this versatile basic sauce any place you'd use a white sauce. Best Foods makes it smooth —you'll make it often, because it's quick! **THIS IS THE PLACE FOR BEST FOODS**

LEMON-Y SAUCE! Combine juice of ½ lemon with 2 tbsp. water or fish stock. Blend with ½ cup Best Foods Real Mayonnaise. salt, pepper. Cook over low heat, just 3 minutes. Stir constantly. Go-with-everything Best Foods makes this sauce combine well with vegetables, fish or meats. Makes you a sauce wizard! **THIS IS THE PLACE FOR BEST FOODS**

109

Quick Stunts with Hunt's TOMATO SAUCE

Oven Barbecue

Wonderful barbecue flavor — quick 'n' easy in your kitchen!

This is a dandy! A real family-pleasing main dish — you can make on the spur of the moment!

You simply take a can of luncheon meat. And Hunt's Tomato Sauce. And combine them—deliciously — in your oven.

The nice, spicy, kettle-simmered flavor of Hunt's Tomato Sauce brings out the smoky goodness of the meat. And, because Hunt's is all tomato, it gives the meat a rich-red glaze. A joy to see — and eat!

You can make so *many* everyday favorites taste wonderful with Hunt's Tomato Sauce. Meatloaf, hamburgers, hash and stew, soups and gravies. Look and see — maybe you could surprise your family with this delicious Oven Barbecue tonight!

1 can luncheon meat	2 Tbsps. brown sugar
1 can Hunt's Tomato Sauce	1 Tbsp. finely grated onion
¼ cup water	¼ teasp. Worcestershire Sauce

Cut meat lengthwise, not quite through, into 8 slices. Place in greased shallow baking dish. Mix Hunt's Tomato Sauce and rest of ingredients. Pour over meat. Bake in hot oven, 425°F., about 30 minutes, basting occasionally. Makes 3 to 4 servings. Double the recipe for larger families. Canned new potatoes are delicious heated and basted along with the meat.

Hunt's
TOMATO SAUCE

Hunt-for the best

Recipes You'll Like on every can of Hunt's Tomato Sauce. Where you shop. Hunt Foods, Inc., Fullerton, Calif.

America's Favorite Tomato Sauce — by far!

110

In an effort to ride the American pizza craze of the 1960s, Hunt's advertised the English muffin pizza, using Hunt's tomato sauce and processed cheese, as an easy alternative to the real thing.

According to the Jell-O Museum website, the people of Salt Lake City consume more lime-flavored gelatin than people in any other city in the United States.

"This Jell-O shortage certainly brings out the artist in me!"

Three spring symphonies, made delicious with Jell-O's "locked-in" flavor: Raspberry Jell-O, half-whipped, half-plain, garnished with maraschino cherries and mint. Lemon and Lime Jell-O, in quivering flakes. A sunshiny dish of fresh oranges molded in Orange Jell-O.

We do not really recommend that one small box of Jell-O be extended to serve, for instance, four tables of bridge.

Still, as long as Jell-O and Jell-O Puddings are still so scarce and precious, the hostess who can make them go far and look gorgeous will continue to get a big hand.

Some day — and it may not be too many months off — the sugar supply will be more plentiful and we can make enough Jell-O products so you can enjoy them any time, on gala days or any day.

Meanwhile, even though you can't make them often, you can always make them fun!

Easter Egg Pudding delights the small fry—cool, satin-smooth Vanilla Pudding decorated with candy eggs in a nest of whipped cream. Another Jell-O Pudding favorite is rich Butterscotch topped with crunchy nut meats.

It's your lucky day when you find yellow-ripe bananas and rich, dark Jell-O Chocolate Pudding to make this company pie. Remember the old-fashioned chocolaty pie grandma used to make? This is it, only more so!

Jell-O is a trade-mark owned by General Foods

PRODUCTS OF GENERAL FOODS

What's found only in Jell-O? That "locked-in" Jell-O Flavor!

JELL-O SIX DELICIOUS FLAVORS

JELL-O PUDDINGS THREE MARVELOUS FLAVORS

Jell-O Puddings—Like Grandma's—only more so!

RECITES

are right in the package...for making delicious

Hot Rolls

and many other fine baked things in

½ **the making time**

(Compared to your standard cookbook recipe)

Now—in far less time—you can make sweet rolls,
dinner rolls, coffee cakes, raised doughnuts,
and other favorites! Just follow Ann Pillsbury's
easy new recipes on the folder inside the package.
Fresh-Acting Yeast is also included, in new,
specially protected yeast packet, to help give you
extra speed and perfect results every time you bake.

*Coffee cakes, sweet rolls,
raised doughnuts, too,
now easy to make. Recipes
for many of your favorites
are on new recipe folder inside the package.*

*You and Ann Pillsbury
can make a great team*

Ann Pillsbury has developed a new hot roll mix
in her kitchen to save you time in your kitchen,
and give you perfect results every time.

3 Original Rogers Silverplated Teaspoons.
Exclusive Lady Ann pattern—only 50c and
6 coupon values. Send to Pillsbury, Box 150,
Minneapolis, Minn. Write for free premium
booklet on Pillsbury Premium Plan. Savings up to
50% on complete silverware service and other valuable articles. Extra-Value coupons with all Pillsbury
packages.

The New, Improved

Pillsbury HOT ROLL MIX

(WITH FRESH-ACTING YEAST)

After a nationwide search, Paul Frees, who voiced the original Boris in *The Adventures of Rocky and Bullwinkle*, beat out 50 actors for the chance to be the voice of the Pillsbury Doughboy in 1965.

To save costs on shipping and reduce breakage, Nebraska native and chemist Edwin Perkins dehydrated his popular Fruit Smack drink in 1927. Later renamed Kool-Aid, it is now the official soft drink of the state of Nebraska.

Refreshments
for
Warm Weather

by Jeanne McCue

It's easy to keep cool and relaxed. Delicious, cooling refreshments like these do the trick. Make them with Kool-Aid in a few minutes. They're amazingly inexpensive. One 5c package of Kool-Aid makes 10 big, cold drinks, or 20 frozen suckers, or 6 heaping servings of luscious frozen dessert. Kool-Aid has been my refreshment standby for years. I keep a liberal supply of all SIX zestful, tangy, Kool-Aid flavors handy in my pantry and a big pitcherful of full-flavored, thirst-quenching Kool-Aid ready in my refrigerator.

Kool-Aid Frozen Desserts

I have a secret recipe for rich dessert, the kind to top off a meal in really grand style. Like all good secrets, it's better when shared. Here it is:

1 package Kool-Aid (any flavor)
1 cup heavy cream
2 cups milk   1 cup sugar

(1) Dissolve Kool-Aid and sugar in milk; turn into freezing tray and freeze ¾ to 1 hour (until slushy). (2) Whip cream (well chilled) until stiff. (3) Add partly frozen Kool-Aid mixture to whipped cream and whip just enough to mix well, but keep as cold as possible. (4) Return quickly to freezing tray and freeze at coldest point. Requires no more stirring. When frozen, set control back to normal. Makes over 1 quart. If desired lighter, beat 2 egg whites fluffy with 2 tablespoons sugar and fold into above mixture before final freezing.

Kool-Aid Frozen Suckers

My neighbor, with five active children, has a real refreshment problem. However, she discovered that the kids will settle for a colorful Kool-Aid frozen sucker any time. See how easy they are to make:

Dissolve thoroughly 1 package Kool-Aid and ⅔ cup sugar in 1 quart water. Pour into cube tray and freeze hard. Remove like ice cubes as wanted, or wrap separately in wax paper and keep in coldest section of freezing compartment. A sucker stick or paper spoon may be frozen in each cube to provide handle.

"Kool-Aid" is a registered trademark of Perkins Products Co.

Copyright, 1949 by Perkins Products Co.

Glamorize it
with the
NEW-DAY
CORN MEAL
with

Fresh Corn Flavor

Quaker
CORN MEAL

Hominy Grits and Quick Grits, too.

Aunt Jemima
CORN MEAL

Hominy Grits, too.

*Look for either of these famous faces
and you get the Fresh Corn Flavor
of choice corn, new milling methods,
new packaging.*

Lazy-Day Beef Pie Dinner

Corn Meal makes the crust both quick and wonderful

It looks glamorous, tastes terrific, takes only 8
minutes to stir up! The trick is to use Quaker (or
Aunt Jemima) Corn Meal . . . the new-day corn
meal that mixes and cooks so quickly, and gives
that wonderful Fresh Corn Flavor! Here's the
tested recipe:

Makes 6 servings

FILLING:
One 1½ lb. can beef stew
One #303 can (about 2 cups)
  peas and carrots, drained
Few drops of spicy hot sauce
CORN BREAD TOPPING:
  1 cup Quaker or Aunt Jemima
  Corn Meal (white or yellow)
2 tablespoons flour
½ teaspoon salt

2 teaspoons baking
  powder
¼ cup chopped
  parsley
¼ cup chopped
  onion
1 egg
½ cup milk
2 tablespoons
  shortening, soft

Mix filling ingredients and place in two-quart
casserole; heat in oven while mixing corn bread.
  For corn bread, sift dry ingredients into bowl.
Stir in parsley and onion. Add egg, milk and
shortening. Beat with rotary beater until well
blended, about 1 minute. *Do not overbeat.* Spoon
batter onto hot meat mixture. Bake in hot oven
(425°F.) about 20 minutes.
  Serve this homey hearty dish tonight. See what
a difference it makes when you use corn meal
with Fresh Corn Flavor!

*P. S. You'll find other quick and easy recipes for tempt-
ing corn meal dishes on every package of Quaker and
Aunt Jemima Corn Meal—Grits, too.*

NEW! The only mix with 25 recipe-ideas in every package!

Pillsbury Hot Roll Mix...

Who says you can't get lots of variety in meatless meals? asked ELSIE, the BORDEN COW

If it's Borden's it's got to be good!

Company lore has it that in 1963, a politician's wife (many think it was Lady Bird Johnson) revealed the secret ingredient in her Texas chili: Ro*Tel Tomatoes and Green Chilies. Ro*Tel is named for Carl Roetelle, who founded the company in the 1940s in Elsa, Texas.

MARY HALE MARTIN stars pineapple in gala treat for the holidays

Libby's Easy-Do Party Tricks

Taste the fresh difference in Libby's

NEW GOLDEN CRISPNESS IN YOUR COOKING
(new flavor, too)

See how golden your pork chops turn out.

...with Kellogg's Corn Flake Crumbs

Somewhere—some time ago—a good cook realized that golden crisp crumbs would make a delicious difference in all kinds of cooking. Soon thousands of smart gals were taking Kellogg's Corn Flakes from the family's breakfast package and rolling them out to use in place of ordinary crumbs.

For all those women—and the thousands who have yet to discover the goodness of Kellogg's Corn Flake Crumbs—here they are, all rolled out for you, especially milled to a fine, even texture for cooking, from Kellogg's famous flakes of corn. Use them often!

Make fried foods more appetizing. These crisp crumbs seal goodness in.

Add flavor in extending meat loaves and patties, coating vegetables and appetizers.

Use in many new ways too . . . such as topping ice cream and in pie crusts.

Attention—Large-Quantity Users: Recipes for 20-100 servings—and Institution-size packages—are available. Write Kay Kellogg, Battle Creek, Michigan.

Kellogg's OF BATTLE CREEK
©1959 by Kellogg Company

BIRDS EYE PEACHES ARE IN!

one of many, many Birds Eye wonder foods—vegetables, poultry, fruits, seafoods!

BARGAIN BUYS IN BIRDS EYE FOODS AT YOUR STORE NOW!

According to Heinz, kids gobble up five billion 1-ounce squirts of ketchup per year. Heinz recently introduced EZ Squirt, fortified with vitamin C and available in red and green varieties.

3 tasty new ways to greet homecomers

PICKLEBURGERS • **ONION-CHEESE PIE** • **CONFETTI BISCUITS**

Sure as there's a nip of autumn in the air, and your family takes to field or stream or football stadium, you can depend on this: they'll come home *ravenous!* You'll especially welcome these new dishes, because they're substantial enough to satisfy the heartiest fall appetites, yet fancy enough for guests. And they're rich with the wonderful homey flavors of Heinz expertly prepared foods! Heinz Condensed Cream of Mushroom Soup contributes its own special creamy richness to Onion-Cheese Pie . . . Crisp, crunchy Heinz Fresh Cucumber Pickle and spicy Heinz Ketchup are two big reasons why Pickleburgers are encore bait. And Confetti Biscuits get their wonderful zest from thick, taste-pleasing Heinz Chili Sauce.

ONION-CHEESE PIE
from Mrs. H. L. Doench, Ferndale, Mich.

Heat oven to 350° F. Line 9-inch pie plate with pastry (using 1 cup flour). Sauté 1 cup thinly sliced or chopped onions in 2 Tbs. butter or margarine until tender. Spread over pastry. Sprinkle with ¾ cup grated American cheese. Blend 3 eggs slightly beaten, 1½ Tbs. flour, 2 tsp. Heinz Mustard. Stir in 1 can (10½ oz.) better-tasting Heinz Condensed Cream of Mushroom Soup, undiluted, and ½ cup milk. Pour over onions. Bake 45 to 60 min. Let stand 10 min. before serving. (Makes 6 tasty, satisfying servings.)

Hearty Fall Luncheon Soup teams *two* Heinz-made favorites: Combine 2 cans (10½ oz.) delicious new Heinz Condensed Minestrone Soup, diluted with equal amt. water, and 1 can (15¼ oz.) energy-packed Heinz Macaroni in smooth cheese sauce. Heat, stirring occasionally. (Makes 5-6 servings.)

Take a Tip from Grandmother! Keep a cruet of Heinz Vinegar (any of the five sparkling, full-flavored kinds) on the table. See what a tempting, new zing it gives to broccoli, cabbage, spinach and other cooked vegetables.

$100 For Recipes. Send us your recipe using any Heinz product. If we use it in our advertising, we'll pay you $100. All recipes become the property of H. J. Heinz Co., and none can be returned. In case of duplicate recipes, naturally only the first one received will be considered. Mail recipe to H. J. Heinz Co., Box 28, LHJ-99, Pittsburgh 30, Pa.

PICKLEBURGERS

Heat oven to 400° F. Shape 1½ lbs. ground beef into 12 thin patties. Sprinkle with salt and pepper. Place an onion slice ¼-inch thick on 6 patties. Divide ⅔ cup Heinz Fresh Cucumber Pickle evenly over onion slices. Top with remaining patties, pressing edges together to seal. Place in shallow pan and bake 10 min. Combine 2 Tbs. water and ½ cup of thick, flavor-coaxing Heinz Ketchup. Spoon over patties. Bake 10 min. Serve in toasted buns. (Makes 6 servings.)

CONFETTI BISCUITS
from Mrs. Walter Mudri, Starford, Pa.

Heat oven to 400° F. Combine 2 cups biscuit mix, ¾ cup grated sharp cheese, 2 Tbs. chopped pimiento, 2 Tbs. chopped green pepper. Stir in ⅔ cup Heinz Chili Sauce (rich with Heinz own pedigreed tomatoes) and ½ cup milk. Beat 15 strokes. Drop from spoon onto greased baking sheet. Bake 12 to 15 min. or until golden brown. Serve with sliced bacon or deviled ham spread. (Makes about 1½ doz. mouth-watering biscuits.)

The sign of good eating

No other Ketchup _tastes_ like Heinz!

You know it's good because it's **Heinz** 57

Miss FLUFFY RICE says:

"EASY, DELICIOUS! VERSATILE, NUTRITIOUS!

RICE

IS YOUR MOST USEFUL FOOD!"

PLAIN OR FANCY—RICE IS SO GOOD. The eating's wonderful with America's good rice! For instance, Heavenly Rice Fluff: Prepare 1 pkg. lemon-flavored gelatin; when partially set, beat until frothy. Whip ½ pt. heavy cream, add ½ cup sugar. Fold into gelatin with 4 cups chilled cooked rice and grated rind of 1 lemon. Mold; chill until set. Serve with raspberries. Serves 6 to 8.

RICE IS SUCH A HELP FOR VARIED MEALS. At breakfast, lunch or dinner—for main course or dessert—there's nothing so versatile as rice. Try it in Ham Roll-Ups: Saute ½ c. each minced green pepper and onion in 2 T. butter for 5 minutes. Mix with 4 cups of hot cooked rice (cook in chicken consommé instead of water). Spread 6 slices of boiled ham with mustard; spoon on rice; roll. Bake, open side down, in a low pan in a 400° oven for 15 minutes.

RICE IS EASY! Today's high quality rice is a breeze to fix—just follow directions on the package. Grown in the USA, the rice you get now is so carefully prepared you don't even have to wash it. Awfully good idea: heat frozen shrimp soup (undiluted) and pour over hot cooked rice.

Start now to discover all that rice can do for you. Versatile, nutritious, and thrifty, too ... rice is your most useful food!

THE RICE INDUSTRY

122

In the 1950s women spent 20 hours per week on food preparation. By 2005 the number had dropped to about 10 hours per week.

Arthur Meyerhoff and Leon Rubin invented PAM, a nonstick cooking spray, in 1957 and sold it commercially for the first time in 1959. PAM is an acronym for "product of Arthur Meyerhoff."

River showboats often stopped at the Higbee plantation and Colonel Higbee entertained the cast. Part of the hospitality was always Aunt Jemima's tender, light and flavorful pancakes, served outdoors, picnic-style.

Aunt Jemima Logo

You can't duplicate it in a homemade batter; you don't get it in any other mix ...

the matchless **4-flour flavor** of Aunt Jemima pancakes

FOR THE FINEST BUCKWHEATS get *Aunt Jemima in the YELLOW box*

The treasured Aunt Jemima recipe combines 4 flours in a special way. **Wheat** flour for lightness, **corn** for tenderness, **rye** for richness, **rice** for browning quality. This 4-flour blend gives Aunt Jemima pancakes a flavor no others can match.

GRIDDLE PICNIC. For informal outdoor eating make "Griddle-burgers" by placing a ground meat patty between two hot Aunt Jemima pancakes. Include "Franks-in-Blankets", by rolling cheese-stuffed frankfurters in hot Aunt Jemima pancakes. Serve with pickles, chili sauce.

Listen to Don McNeill's Breakfast Club ABC radio and TV, weekdays

Best Cooks way to delicious QUICK MEALS

STOKELY'S *Finest* **TOMATO JUICE**
gives a lift to any meal

STOKELY'S *Finest* **CATSUP**
is so good you'll pour it on

STOKELY'S .. FOR THE FINEST IN FRUITS AND VEGETABLES · VAN CAMP'S .. THE LARGEST SELLING BEANS IN THE WORLD

Stokely–Van Camp

In 1956 Maxim's of Paris introduced frozen prepared meals for sale in stores under the Maxim's brand. Almost 40 years later, in 2002, Wolfgang Puck introduced a line of wood-fired frozen pizzas.

Earl Tupper introduced his first lidded bowls—inspired by airtight cans of paint—in 1946. The bowls weren't big sellers until he introduced the Tupperware Home Party in 1948, offering women the opportunity to sell the plastic products in their homes and to befriend their neighbors.

3 SOUPER SALADS

Make 'em the easy way...with soup!

They're cool. They're quick. They're creamy-delicious. Wonderful soup salads! You make them first thing in the morning (or even the night before) . . . and you make them with soup for extra-rich flavor, subtle wake-up seasonings. Then into the refrigerator. And no matter how high the mercury climbs, your family has a taste-tempting treat when dinnertime comes around. Try a cool-off salad soon.

Creamy Tuna Salad. Sprinkle 1 env. unflavored gelatine on ½ cup cold water to soften; place over boiling water; stir until gelatine is dissolved. Blend 1 can Campbell's Cream of Celery Soup with a 3-oz. pkg. cream cheese; add dissolved gelatine, a 7-oz. can tuna (drained and flaked), ½ cup shredded carrot, ½ cup chopped celery, 2 tbsp. chopped parsley, 1 tbsp. lemon juice. Pour into 1-qt. mold. Chill until firm. Unmold; serve on crisp salad greens. 4 servings.

Ham-Macaroni Salad. Combine 1 can Campbell's Cream of Chicken Soup, ¼ cup chopped celery, ¼ cup chopped onion, 2 tbsp. chopped green pepper, ½ tsp. prepared mustard, dash Tabasco, dash pepper. Stir in 2 cups cooked macaroni (4 oz. uncooked) and 1 cup diced cooked ham. Chill. Serve with tomato wedges. 4 to 6 servings.

Shrimp Lamaze. Blend 1 can Campbell's Tomato Soup with 1 cup mayonnaise. Add ¼ cup sweet-pickle relish, ¼ tsp. grated onion, ½ tsp. prepared mustard, and 1 tbsp. lemon juice. Makes about 2½ cups dressing. Serve over cooked shrimp. Or try with lettuce wedges, hard-cooked eggs or mixed greens. Delicious every way!

Look for other easy recipes on the back of every can.

Good things begin to happen when you cook with *Campbell's Soup*

129

CHAPTER 4

One-Hit Wonders:
Unforgettable Products and Ingredients

Flipping through women's magazines from the 1940s, 1950s, and 1960s, it's easy to imagine just how overwhelmed shoppers must have been by the pages upon pages of advertisements, touting a larder's worth of new ingredients that lured women into the promised land of convenience and cooking ease. With all the choices suddenly available to them, it's a wonder dinner ever got made at all. Advertising had to work harder to make products unique and to appear to deliver even more value for consumers. In an early foreshadowing of nutraceuticals, Tang with Bufferin hit the market in the mid-1960s, combining astronaut-approved orange flavor with a pain reliever (perhaps designed to quell the many headaches housekeeping could produce).

But more than headache relief, what moms really sought was something to put the zing back into their kitchen routines. Cooking needed to become fun, and convenience foods were just the ticket. Manufacturers answered the call, introducing newfangled products and, equally important, positioning old staples in new ways. Developing easy, crowd-pleasing recipes had always been a sure-fire way to engender consumer loyalty, and at the height of the convenience-food renaissance, instructions for potato salad, ham sandwiches, and Rice Krispies treats were pared down to the bare minimum, sometimes calling for little more than three ingredients and three steps. In effect, this changed the definition of "recipes" forever and foreshadowed the popularity of three-, four-, and five-ingredient cookbooks today.

Other incentives attempted to appeal to a time-tested love of gadgets, gimmicks, and special promotions. The prospect of a free cookbook, discounted salad spinner, or kitschy-cute sauce warmer helped distinguish one item from the next, and they had women eagerly awaiting the daily mail delivery. Also helping forge

identities between competitors were catchy advertising campaigns and slogans. "Libby, Libby, Libby on the Label, Label, Label" rolled off the tongue as smoothly as a canned cling peach, and when you "bring out the Best Foods" (or Hellman's, if you were east of the Mississippi), you "bring out the best." There wasn't a dish in the 1950s kitchen that didn't love mayonnaise; it was the condiment that seemed to last forever in the fridge once opened. In an early ad Best Foods told women that store-bought mayo was better than homemade, since the salad oil was fresher.

But soon versatility, not freshness, became its selling point as food stylists and recipe mavens concocted ever-stranger uses for the creamy condiment. Aside from making friends with slices of Wonder bread and chopped chicken, mayo was seen keeping company with a green gelatin, cozying up to ketchup and relish to make Thousand Island dressing, and making fast friends with grapefruit segments. These jars, bottles, boxes, and packets were just the ticket for American housewives pining for dinnertime inspiration. The alluringly designed packaging helped products vie for their mistress's adoration, with creative menu ideas straight out of the mind of a slightly unstable food stylist. What else could explain a Miracle Whip's promise that "only Miracle Whip can make pears taste so good"? The pitiful pear pictured in the ad was cosseted by a frill of impossibly green lettuce and spackled with a dollop of the creamy condiment, which had originally been invented during the Great Depression as a cheaper alternative to egg-rich mayonnaise. They called it a salad; we detect the machinations of a lazy test-kitchen chef. Every food genre, from appetizer to dessert, was fair game for the maraschino-cherry-and-mayo marketers, who forged food products into advertising gold. A New England housewife broke up some baking chocolate to make cookies, and Toll House morsels were born. Del Monte romanced women with the idea of "turning crackers into cake" by crumbling soda crackers mixed with sugar and margarine on top of a can of its fruit cocktail. Hunt's slathered bacon-wrapped hot dogs with tomato sauce and called it an innovation. These were combinations developed by marketers and embraced by a population eager for variety. On their own, many of these products were mere bit players in the convenience kitchen, but when they joined forces, they could create unforgettable no-muss, no-fuss dishes. They were, in effect, the building blocks of a dinner beautification project that could be undertaken with ease. Just open, pour, mix, stir, or heat...and presto!

Even snack-time got the quick 'n' easy treatment, with popcorn taking the lead. Indiana native Frederick Mennen worked for five years to get kernels to pop just right, but his corn didn't sell in its original cans. Mennen came up with the idea of enclosing the kernels in an aluminum pan covered with foil and attaching a wire handle to the circular disc. Jiffy Pop debuted in 1959 and became the unofficial TV-watching snack of a newly minted generation of boob-tube-obsessed kids who loved to watch as the popcorn pan turned into a billowing dome.

The Oscar Mayer Wienermobile was built in 1936 at a cost of $5,000 and was introduced in Chicago to promote the company's German-style wieners. Today's Wienermobile has a wireless microphone system, GPS navigational system, and a removable bun roof.

Turn leftover meat into "company hash"

with Grandma Snider's real Country-Style Catsup

made with Super Tomatoes

Give your salads a helping hand

with quality-famous Ann Page Dressings

Your friendly A&P

AMERICA'S DEPENDABLE FOOD MERCHANT SINCE 1859

Deliciously yours!

There never were exactly 57 varieties of Heinz products. Founder Henry John Heinz liked the numbers 5 and 7 and strung them together to create his company's famous slogan.

It's 8 flavors tastier than any single juice!

The way many people rave about the flavor of **V-8***, you'd think it was ice cream, cake, and Grandma's apple pie all rolled into one.

But delicious flavor isn't the only attraction of this remarkable 8-juice blend. It's brimful of vitamins .. rich with minerals ... and so low in calories you'll never go to waist drinking it.

No *single* juice (vegetable *or* fruit) can equal **V-8** for flavor or health. Enjoy its refreshment today.

**V-8 is a trademark owned by the makers of Campbell's Soups*

V-8's magic blend: the juices of the Campbell Tomato, celery, carrots, beets, spinach, lettuce, watercress, and parsley.

By Nature it's wholesome ... by *Campbell's* it's delicious!

Just taste them all together

Creamy smooth whole-egg mayonnaise
blends them into a perfect WALDORF SALAD!

Taste each distinctive flavor at its best in a
Waldorf Salad. Each is enhanced by the delicate
touch of whole-egg mayonnaise. Hellmann's and
Best Foods is made with freshly broken whole eggs
— whites, yolks, even extra yolks. Made truly
creamy, truly smooth, no delicate in taste . . .
always just right for all your mayonnaise needs.

To bring out the Whole Flavor use *Real* Whole-Egg Mayonnaise . . .
creamy smooth **Best Foods'** or **HELLMANN'S**

EVERYWOMAN'S • OCTOBER 1953

Young actor (and future president)
Ronald Reagan began advertising
V-8 juice in magazines in 1948.

HOW 12/16/51

Ronald Reagan
discovered **V-8***

has Lively Flavor
and Goodness no <u>single</u>
juice can match!

V8 FOR VITAMINS
FOR VITALITY

"V-8 Vegetable Juices
is a delicious blend of
8 juices in one drink!"

Ronald Reagan
Starring in
"HONG KONG"
Color by Technicolor
A Pine–Thomas Paramount Picture

Turn vegetables into a treat!
Cheez Whiz 'em

Just spoon some Kraft's Cheez Whiz into a sauce pan and put it over very low heat (or use the top of a double boiler). Either way this amazing pasteurized process cheese spread gives you wonderful cheese sauce fast without fuss. A flavor lift that takes vegetables out of the "daily" class—makes 'em a treat. Here so have hot Cheez Whiz for cooked, drained cauliflower and green beans, with broiled tomato halves.

More speedy tricks: Spoon Cheez Whiz right into hot foods—such as mashed potatoes. And for snacks and sandwiches, spread it. Cheez Whiz gives you dozens of fast cheese treats.

Onions à la Cheez Whiz. Put Cheez Whiz in a pan over very low heat, or the top of a double boiler. Pour the smooth cheese sauce over drained, hot cooked onions.

Best broccoli ever? No need to fuss with a heavy sauce. Pour on plenty of hot Cheez Whiz and taste what that tantalizing cheese flavor does for drained, hot cooked broccoli.

NEW! PIMENTO CHEEZ WHIZ

"Let's have Sandwiches
...WITH THAT FRENCH'S FLAVOR!"

French's Mustard is Smoother, Creamier—

MILLIONS PREFER ITS FINER FLAVOR!

Double or triple decker? Get out this trayful of delectable "fixings" and let everyone have the fun of making his own favorite sandwich. And to be sure your sandwich tray's a hit, serve plenty of French's—the smooth delicious mustard that brings out all the superb flavor of meat, cheese or fish. French's blends is perfectly—it's made of the finest spices and mustard seed money can buy!

Largest selling prepared mustard in the U.S.A. today

FREE! Hot Dan's new Recipe Book in full color... "Mealtime Magic"
Send coupon to The R. T. French Company, 964 Mustard Street, Rochester 9, N. Y.

The good news is spreading!

Blue Plate Mayonnaise is *lower* in saturated fat than the leading refrigerated spreads. It's the only mayonnaise made with 100 per cent pure vegetable oil from Wesson. Next time—spread on the good taste of Blue Plate.

After being introduced in 1928, Velveeta processed cheese was the first cheese product to be approved by the American Medical Association. Velveeta was later reformulated as a cheese spread in 1953.

According to a survey cited in a U.S. Department of Agriculture study, only 55 percent of American dinners contain one or more homemade dish.

Largest selling prepared mustard in the U. S. A. today

America's
wonderful crackers are
extra good when you

Cheez Whiz 'em!

Hungry for a snack? Or—do you need a whole company tray? Just reach for several packages of your favorite crackers and your jar of Cheez Whiz.

With a quick swish of the knife you put tantalizing cheese goodness on crackers when you Cheez Whiz 'em. Keep a jar of Kraft's amazing pasteurized process cheese spread on hand for really great cheese 'n cracker snacks . . . and for dozens of other fast cheese treats, too.

Spread it! *for snacks*
Heat it! *for cheese sauce*
Spoon it! *on hot foods*

KRAFT'S
Cheez Whiz
For Fast Cheese Treats
A PASTEURIZED PROCESS CHEESE SPREAD

In the early 1930s Kraft began selling its cheese spreads in brightly colored, reusable glass jars called Swanky Swigs to distinguish its products from similar ones made by competitors.

Elsie, the Borden milk products mascot, was so popular in 1948 that more people could identify her than Republican presidential candidate Thomas Dewey.

The most wonderful thing has happened to cream cheese !

New Borden Formula Guarantees a Freshness, Flavor, and Texture That Cream Cheese Never Had Before

There's just one thing for you to do!

Get down to your food store as fast as your legs can carry you and buy at least one 3-oz. package of the new Borden's Cream Cheese!

Made in a brand-new way by a new formula, Borden's tastes better than any cream cheese you know. Fresh and delicate—a flavor that teases and tempts you!

The texture is entirely new. Lighter, fluffier. It breaks cleanly, doesn't crumble. It's smooth . . . spreads easily.

One taste, and you'll be making excuses to eat Borden's Cream Cheese every day . . . so try these ideas:

* * *

Berry and Cream Cheese Salad: Place a ring of golden pineapple on crisp salad greens and crown it with a generous chunk of the new Borden's Cream Cheese. Garnish with sliced fresh strawberries. Superb!

Springtime Sandwich Assortment: Make the most delicious sandwiches for parties, picnics, or lunch boxes with Borden's Cream Cheese . . .

. . . by itself, on date and nut bread;
. . . on rye bread, with chopped chives or avocado;
. . . on white bread, with mint jelly or marmalade;
. . . on whole wheat, with chutney or India relish.

* * *

Get Borden's Cream Cheese from the dairy case at your store today . . . in 3-oz. or 8-oz. packages. It's always *fresh.* Borden's Cheese distributors see to that! And it's made and packed to keep fresh longer!

In fact we're so convinced that Borden's Cream Cheese is the best you ever ate, we've put an *absolute guarantee* on every package. If for any reason you're not satisfied, return it to your store for full credit!

Borden's Fine Cheeses
Folks who know cheese say "Borden's please!"

Best behaved cheese you ever cooked with !

Here's one cheese food that has real character in the flavor! Slices clean when cold. Cooks superbly. Never strings nor curdles! It's Borden's Chateau—the finest cheese food for cheese dreams, sauces, and cooked cheese dishes . . . for cold plates and sandwiches, too. At your store. ½-lb. package (plain or pimento) or 2-lb. loaf. **ST. M. Reg. U. S. Pat. Off.**

Folks can't seem to get enough of this !

Borden's Gruyere is a delicate, delicious Swiss process cheese with a nut-sweet flavor. Grand for dessert, for snacks with rounds of Melba toast or crackers, and mighty welcome in a lunch box. © The Borden Company

Reminder-add these to your shopping list !

Four more of more than forty cheeses that Borden's makes for cheese-lovers! Borden's offers you more fine perishable cheese specialties than any other cheese maker. Shop for them in the dairy case at your store.

ONCE AGAIN KRAFT MAKES AN IMPORTANT IMPROVEMENT IN MARGARINE FLAVOR!

NEW
SWEET CHILLED
PARKAY

You'll discover a wonderful change has been made in Parkay Margarine! Each
package of New Parkay is *sweet chilled* before the handy sticks are molded and
wrapped. And the special way in which Parkay is sweet chilled keeps its delightful
flavor uniform in quality over many weeks. You'll enjoy Parkay's delectable taste.
You'll like the way it spreads. New Sweet Chilled Parkay spreads smoothly even
when ice cold. Your grocer has New Sweet Chilled Parkay now. Try it soon.

Threatened by the ascent of butter substitutes, dairy farmers successfully lobbied for the passage of federal margarine taxes. Instituted in 1885, the taxes were not repealed until 1951. In 1930 per capita consumption of margarine was 2.6 pounds; today it is 8.3 pounds.

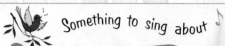
Something to sing about ♪

New Springtime-Flavor NUCOA
Now America's Most Delicious Spread

Here's the spread that gives you the sweet, wholesome freshness of Springtime- all year round!

Here's the first and only spread to combine welcome economy, unsurpassed year-round nutrition, and the magical flavor that is Nucoa's alone! On breads, it is so fresh, so sweet! As a seasoning, so rich, so flavorful. Use it in *all* cooking, for baking, for frying. Yes! New Nucoa margarine is everything you ever dreamed of in a spread . . . America's most delicious. Try it today!

ONE POUND NET WEIGHT

NUCOA ★ 4 QUARTERS

YELLOW

4 QUARTER POUND YELLOW PRINTS

OLEOMARGARINE

"NUCOA" REG. U. S. PAT. OFF.

For more flavor, more color, more vitamins, serve your vegetables with a big pat of golden Nucoa.

In those states where the ban on yellow margarine has not yet been lifted, enjoy fresh, rich Nucoa in the handy Measure-Pak.

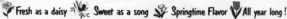
Fresh as a daisy ❋ Sweet as a song 🌹 Springtime Flavor All year long !

What a Peanut Butter! So nourishing a sandwich equals a square meal!

Big Top

It's naturally fortified!

NUTRITIONISTS AGREE: One Big Top sandwich has as much basic nourishment—proteins, fats, carbohydrates, food energy—as this meal of lamb chop, potato, green beans.

We're not suggesting that you give up hot dishes and serve Big Top sandwiches for every meal. But when you want a quick, delicious lunch or snack, it's good to know: Big Top peanut butter is naturally fortified —a *powerhouse of nourishment*. Just one sandwich (1½ ounces of Big Top) has as much basic food value as the meal above, with normal portions shown. All this *plus* important vitamins and minerals.

Enjoy creamy, easy-spreading Big Top between two slices of bread—a glass of milk— fresh fruit. Mmm, what a lunch!

© W. T. Young Foods, Inc., subsidiary of Procter & Gamble

"We're hungry as bears"
says your gang home at four
Serve 'em BIG TOP —
for golden-good taste they'll adore!

Comes in exclusive
"Early American" goblets
and sherbets, in addition to
the handy refrigerator jar

According to the Skippy website, Americans eat about three pounds of peanut butter per person each year, which is enough peanut butter to cover the floor of the Grand Canyon.

Arachibutyrophobia is the fear of peanut butter getting stuck to the roof of your mouth.

America's Favorite Peanuts
now come to you in

America's *Handiest* Can!

Another PLANTERS First

Only PLANTERS give you those crisp, top quality Salted Peanuts that the whole world loves—big, selected Virginia peanuts—roasted and salted to flavor peak.

And only PLANTERS gives you this wonderful new coaster-top vacuum can—the handiest you ever saw. No more raw, sharp edges; instead the lid edge is safely rounded and fits down *inside* the can as a snug-fitting cover. You'll love both the peanuts and the can. Get PLANTERS today!

Use as a Coaster . . . You'll like this feature. Each lid is shaped and ridged to make a handy coaster for long, cool drinks.

MIXED NUTS
De Luxe Mixture—all high grade nuts; vacuum-packed; salted and roasted to PLANTERS perfection.

5¢ BAG
The famous "Nickel Lunch" . . . energy & vitamins plus.

JUMBO BLOCK
Pure peanut candy at its wholesome, delicious best. Still only 5¢.

PEANUT BUTTER
Super-smooth—Chill Packed for easy spreading and rich, old-fashioned flavor that really tastes like peanuts.

Also in 12 oz. screw-cup refrigerator-freezer jar

COOKING and SALAD OIL
The truly all purpose oil for better deep and pan frying—baking—salads. No peanut taste, but it enhances flavors of other foods.

A wonderful new Adventure in Good Cooking!

How to make family and guests say, "M-m-m. This tastes so-o-o good!"

You never saw a cookbook quite like this one. Over 100 new recipes with scores of variations, ranging all 'round the menu; special Italian and Oriental recipes; fascinating appetizers and snacks; party suggestions for easy entertaining; new cooking techniques. Many pictures in full color. Enclose just 10¢ to cover handling and mailing cost. *Mail coupon today!*

These PLANTERS Products are also made in Toronto and sold everywhere in Canada

MR. PEANUT

PLANTERS *is the word for good* PEANUTS

Popcorn was the first food used to test microwave rays in 1946.

Born in 1907, Orville Redenbacher was always obsessed with popcorn. He even experimented on it in college. In 1965, at the age of 58, Redenbacher developed a proprietary 44:1 expansion ratio for light and fluffy popcorn. In 1971 he started the famous company that bears his name. Redenbacher died in 1995.

After Pop-Tart lover Thomas Nangle's toaster oven erupted in flames in 1992 and he threatened to sue the Kellogg's corporation, a Texas A&M professor conducted a series of independent tests that proved that a Pop-Tart can produce 18-inch flames within 40 seconds of ignition. Kellogg's settled out of court with Nangle.

Scrumptious new Lucky Whip dessert topping tastes like it's homemade

—yet contains only <u>18 calories</u> per average serving

A luscious new dessert topping is now in your grocer's refrigerated case. It's called Lucky Whip. And it really tastes like it's homemade.

Our photo shows what it can do for short-cake. *True luxury.* Surprisingly, Lucky Whip is low in calories. Only 18 calories per average serving. (If you want a double serving, shucks, that's only 36 calories.)

The old-fashioned kinds come in small six-ounce cans. Lucky Whip comes in a giant can. You and your family get as many as ten extra servings.

Crown your family's desserts with Lucky Whip—scrumptious on pies, puddings, ice cream, cakes. All your favorite desserts. Lucky Whip® is guaranteed by Lever Brothers to taste like it's homemade—or your money back.

154

How to Make Strawberries SING!

Serve 'em with *Reddi-wip*

YOUR FIRST TASTE WILL TELL YOU *it's whipped cream*

The first aerosol-can for cooking sprays had to battle the public's association with insecticide, which had been sold in similar packaging. People didn't accept this new form of packing until Reddi-wip whipped cream came on the market and became an instant favorite.

SHORTCUT TO SHORTCAKE...

Take your favorite shortcake, dessert shells or biscuits, add red-ripe strawberries, and crown with a snowy swirl of Reddi-Wip... so easy and so delicious because Reddi-Wip is *real* cream flavored with just a hint of sugar and vanilla.

Never a Lump

en you make <u>Cream Sauce</u> with

TTER-BLENDING Carnation

Smoothest cream sauce you ever made! Quickest, too! That's because Carnation has special blending qualities not found in any other form of milk. And because it's double-rich—you need only half as much flour and shortening.

For better results at less cost, cook with THE MILK THAT WHIPS

Carnation
EVAPORATED
MILK

Give all your baking this "golden goodness"

Instant shortening! Golden Mazola® Oil is fast changing old-fashioned baking habits!

New! Our quick 'n easy NO-ROLL PIE CRUST make it right in the pie pan!

Mazola
the golden oil
for frying...
salads...baking

Mazola

Drink this hearty coffee as strong as you like

It still can't get on your nerves! Drink as many cups as you like ... as often as you like ... Sanka still can't make you jittery or keep you awake. All pure coffee. 97% caffein-free.

NEW INSTANT SANKA COFFEE

SANKA COFFEE

The same fudge recipe—made with marshmallow cream and chocolate chips—has appeared on the back of Marshmallow Fluff jars since 1956.

Fudge in 5 minutes! No Beating! No Failures!

Carnation is the secret – ordinary milk won't do

So easy–no soft ball tests or candy thermometer needed. And *so smooth*–thanks to special blending qualities of Carnation *not found in any other form of milk.*

FREE! Send today for "Party Sweets," booklet of new desserts, icings, candies. Address Mary Blake, Carnation Co., Dept. LM-125. Los Angeles 36. Calif. **ENJOY** Burns and Allen on CBS-TV every week.

CARNATION 5-MINUTE FUDGE

Mix ⅔ cup undiluted Carnation Evaporated Milk, 1⅔ cups sugar and ½ teaspoon salt in saucepan over low heat. Heat to boiling, then cook 5 minutes, stirring constantly. Remove from heat.

Add 1½ cups (16 medium) diced marshmallows, 1½ cups semi-sweet chocolate pieces, 1 teaspoon vanilla, ½ cup chopped nuts. Stir 1-2 minutes (until marshmallows melt). Pour into buttered 9″ square pan.

Carnation
EVAPORATED MILK

"from Contented Cows"

For a better cup of coffee, "cream" it with Carnation—THE MILK THAT WHIPS!

157

These biscuits were made with another shortening and baked 15 minutes at 425 degrees oven heat. Compare their appearance with the biscuits on the right.

These biscuits were made with golden Fluffo from the same recipe and baked for the same length of time at the same heat as the biscuits on the left.

Something Golden Happens

(golden fluffiness you've never gotten with any other shortening)

Pure shortening, not a table spread.
Golden yellow from pure, wholesome carotene.

Expect surprising results when you use Fluffo; it's an altogether surprising shortening. To make it, we had to break down old-style shortening to its very molecules, and improve them; it takes the cream of the crop to make golden Fluffo.

No other leading shortening gives you such light, fluffy, golden-brown biscuits, golden yellow inside even before you butter them. No change in your recipe —just a wonderful change in results.

No other kind of shortening gives you such crisp, light, golden-brown fried foods. Everything fried right and light in Fluffo is beautifully browned all over—and just as digestible as it looks.

Fluffo even handles differently; it's so much lighter and fluffier it's a joy to use. Blends with fewer, easier strokes, and the golden color lets you see how perfectly you're mixing cake batter or pie dough. Try golden Fluffo; how can you possibly miss?

Convenience foods broadcast their way to popularity by sponsoring top TV shows. Fluffo shortening and Sanka instant coffee sponsored *I Love Lucy.*

Makeup artists often use Karo corn syrup cut with red food coloring as a stand-in for blood on TV and movie sets.

"...the power behind the home"

"...Gran'ma told me that Karo has been a stand-by in her house for 35 years...and Mom says she's been serving Karo in hundreds of ways ever since she and Dad were married.

Me...I began life on Karo. Right now, I get Karo in some way every day...it makes so many foods taste swell...and don't Doctors say it's good for growing children...'cause it's so rich in dextrose, food-energy sugar?

How do I look, Folks...strong and healthy?"

THE KARO KID

Foods for growing children made more nutritious and delicious with Karo

 ARO ON CEREALS—DELICIOUS! Blue Label Karo provides necessary energy sugar which young children, as well as babies, need abundantly. Karo supplies the sweets required by your growing child, without forming the "sweet-tooth" habit. Let youngsters pour from their own pitcher of Karo. It's good for them. *Also...*children need no coaxing to drink milk fortified with Karo.

 TEMPTING BAKED CUSTARD. Whip together 3 *large eggs;* add ⅓ *cup Blue Label Karo,* pinch *salt,* 1 *tsp. vanilla.* Stir in 2¾ *cups hot milk,* mix well. Place ⅓ *tbsp. Karo,* in each of 6 custard cups. Fill with custard mixture; place in a pan of warm water, bake in slow oven (300 to 325°F.) for 45 minutes. Also Karo is delicious on corn starch or rice puddings, rennet and gelatin desserts.

ICHER FLAVORED BAKED APPLES. Place 6 *cored apples* in baking dish. Put 1 *tbsp. Karo* in each apple. Mix ½ *cup Blue Label Karo* and ⅓ *cup water* and baste over apples as they bake in a hot oven (400°F.) for 45 minutes. Pears, bananas, peaches may be baked deliciously with 2 parts Karo to 1 of water.

OMPH FOR STEWED FRUITS! Blue Label Karo improves texture and adds flavor to dried, stewed fruits such as prunes, peaches, pears, apples, apricots. Simmer ¼ *lb. dried fruit* with 1⅓ *cups water,* ¼ *cup Karo,* in covered pan till tender. Serves 4.

Karo is rich in dextrose . . . food-energy sugar

*Free—*A NEW, SPECIAL BOOKLET

Containing dozens of tested recipes for appetizing, nutritious treats for growing children . . . delicious desserts, tempting cereals, puddings, custards, approved party foods and beverages. Just send postcard with your name and address to Corn Products Sales Company, Dept. B2, Box 36, Station P, New York 4, N. Y.

©C.P.S.Co.

Hershey's chocolate syrup was introduced as an industrial product for bakeries and factories in 1926. By 1928 a home version in a can hit the market. The packaging remained the same until 1968, when a lid was added to lock in freshness.

In 1949 Charles Lubin named his company's now-famous cheesecake after his eight-year-old daughter, Sara Lee.

In 1978 Dan White was acquitted in the murder of San Francisco mayor George Moscone and city supervisor Harvey Milk after using the "Twinkie defense," claiming the sugar and additives in processed foods further deepened the depression that led to his actions. The controversy didn't affect the pastries. According to its website, Interstate Bakeries, the makers of Twinkies, is the largest wholesale baker and distributor of fresh baked bread and sweet goods.

Chocolate Chip Cookies

*You can't match the kind
you make with Baker's Chocolate Chips!*

One taste will tell you why Baker's Chocolate Chips are best for cookies. The flavor's so much richer! These semi-sweet chips are made from Baker's Chocolate—finest in the world! And they keep their shape through baking! Make sure you get Baker's Chocolate Chips. Can't-fail cookie recipe on package.

Walter
BAKER'S
SEMI-SWEET
Chocolate Chips

Chocolate makes it good ... Baker's makes it best

Chocolate Marshmallow Cake

Top a devil's food cake with marshmallow whip and chocolate frosting. And remember—only Baker's Chocolate makes the cake and frosting so dark, so delicious! Recipes' on package of superb Baker's Unsweetened Chocolate—America's favorite for almost 2 centuries!

Products of General Foods

**BAKER'S
CHOCOLATE**

BAKER'S CHOCOLATE

Everybody goes for Crispy Treats

"Rice Krispies" is a Trademark (Reg. U.S. Pat. Off.) of the Kellogg Company for its oven-popped rice

Make 'em in six minutes with
Kellogg's RICE KRISPIES and MARSHMALLOWS

Serve up some Marshmallow Crispy Treats and little hands will clean the plate quicker'n you can fill it. And that's fast. Because you can heap a platter in the time it takes to count leisurely to 360. What do you need? Kellogg's Rice Krispies, butter, marshmallows and six minutes' time.

Bet you know some little kiddies who'd love to be sweetened right now. So why not make for the kitchen and make ready some of these crispy candy treats?

HERE'S HOW TO MAKE MARSHMALLOW CRISPY TREATS

¼ cup butter or margarine
½ pound (about 32) marshmallows
5 cups KELLOGG'S RICE KRISPIES

1. Melt butter in 3-quart saucepan. Add marshmallows and cook over low heat, stirring constantly, until marshmallows are melted and mixture is well-blended. Remove from heat.

2. Add Rice Krispies and stir until well-coated with marshmallow mixture.

3. Press warm marshmallow crispy mixture lightly into buttered 13 x 9-inch pan. Cut into squares when cool. Yield: 24 2-inch squares.

NOTE: 2 cups (1 1-pint jar) marshmallow crème may be substituted for marshmallows. Cook over low heat about 6 minutes, stirring constantly.

In 1933 Snap! Krackle! and Pop! first began voicing the sound that Kellogg's Rice Krispies make when combined with milk.

In 1959 sales of packaged cranberries dropped precipitously after the U.S. government falsely reported that a weed killer associated with cranberry crops was poisonous.

HERE'S WHY I INSIST ON CERTO

...THE "TRIED AND TRUE" PECTIN THAT TAKES THE GUESSWORK OUT OF JELLY-MAKING

says *Mrs. F. B. Tillou, Jr.*
of Oxford, New Jersey, veteran Jelly Champion who has won over 150 prizes for jams and jellies made with Certo!

Watch Mrs. Tillou demonstrate to her neighbors how Certo saves time, money and work!

1. **"There's no excuse** for jelly failure nowadays," says Mrs. Tillou. "With Certo, any woman can make *perfect* jelly from any fruit she sets her hand to—even hard-to-jell fruits like strawberries and pineapple.

2. **"No slaving over a hot stove**—when you use Certo. For Certo cuts down the boiling time to ½ minute for jellies—only a minute or so for jams. You're through in just 15 minutes from the time your fruit was prepared.

3. **"11 glasses instead of 7—** and all from only 4 cups of juice! You can see for yourself that Certo gives you actually half again more jam or jelly. For due to that short ½ minute boil, no costly fruit juices get boiled off in steam.

A product of General Foods

4. **"Better tasting jams and jellies** you never ate! That short boil saves more than juice, you know. It saves flavor, too—so jams and jellies made with Certo retain the delicious flavor of the fresh, ripe fruit itself. And Certo alone gives you 79 recipes—*another* important reason why jelly champions insist on this 'tried and true' pectin!"

Look for the tested recipes under the label of every bottle of Certo.

4 *SPEED-UP* SALADS

with sunny **CLING PEACHES** and creamy **COTTAGE CHEESE**
serve crisp, golden Fritos® on the side

TWO-MINUTE FAMILY BOWL! Want to watch your weight? Please someone small? Dazzle extra-special company? Then heap snowy mounds of cottage cheese in your showiest salad bowl, and ring it 'round with golden cling peaches. Garnish with romaine spears or celery sticks—and in two minutes, you've got the salad all America loves best! 'Specially tasty with crisp, crunchy Fritos corn chips on the side!

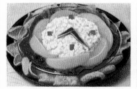

TIMELY LUNCH IDEA! Ring cottage cheese with plump cling peach slices. Now make clock hands with green pepper strips; mark hours with pimento.

QUICK FUN FARE FOR SMALL FRY! Catch compliments with a golden cling "sunfish"! Save wedge for the tail; garnish with olive slice.

A BREEZE TO FIX! It's a Sailboat Salad, with a green pepper-pimento boat on a sea of cottage cheese. Add clings and watch folks sail into it!

ONE MINUTE, PLEASE! To make sure you turn out a triumph of a salad, you'll want the sunniest, shapeliest, showiest peaches you can find. And that's just what you'll get when you choose *clings!*

Canned *Cling Peaches* from California

Cling Peach Advisory Board

170

During World War II apple shortages drove the Ritz cracker company to develop a recipe for mock apple pie that is still used today.

YIP! IT MIXES INSTANTLY IN COLD MILK

YIPPEE! IT'S EXTRA CHOCOLATY

Nestlé's Quik!

Everybody goes for extra quick, extra delicious Nestlé's Quik. Just 2 heaping teaspoons of Quik powder change plain cold milk into a chocolate-rich drink. A stir mixes it, keeps it mixed all the way down. Your kids will drink more milk when it's QUIK-mixed.

Steig

Grown-Ups too,
love a chocolaty
"Quik-Me-Up"
you never knew milk could
taste so good!

Wake up to TANG

[N]ew breakfast drink discovery with [m]ore vitamin C than orange juice!

[There]'s no summer vacation from your need for vitamin C. You need it every [day of] the year. You can't store it up for tomorrow.

[Tang] provides more vitamin C than fresh or frozen orange or grapefruit juice, [more] protective vitamin A, too, than tomato juice.

[And TANG is instant.] No spurting, no unboxing, TANG's fresh wake-up taste [comes out in plain cold water—always golden-good, never acid.] Keep [plenty] on hand. It really puts the "good" in "Good Morning"!

NEW! INSTANT

Originally released by General Foods in 1957, Tang was a commercial failure until NASA adopted the powdered orange drink as a beverage on Gemini flights in 1965.

Nestlé's Quik, the first powdered chocolate milk mix, was developed in the United States in 1948.

Which popular breakfast drink gives you the most Vitamin C?

Easy answer: Tang. Here are the facts: Tang is not a juice or a juice product—it comes in instant form. It has natural orange flavor. *And* it has more protective Vitamin C than either orange *or* tomato juice. Ounce for ounce. Glass for glass. This is the big reason Tang is a favorite breakfast drink in so many thoughtful families these days.

Other reasons: Tang is remarkably convenient. You mix only what you need, fresh every morning. And, in addition to having more Vitamin C, glass for glass, than orange juice, Tang is more economical, too.

Maybe you've been missing something at breakfast. Maybe it's Tang.

GENERAL FOODS KITCHENS

Conclusion

Fifty years after "heat it and eat it" entered the American vocabulary, it's clear that convenience foods aren't a craze—they're a kitchen mainstay. Designed to make our lives easier, they've also made millionaires out of those smart enough to realize that as much as good taste matters, so does saving time. Convenience foods endured as a cultural litmus test, adapting to the needs of society and reflecting trends beyond the kitchen. Women entered the workforce en masse in the late 1960s and the 1970s, motivated both by the prospect of an identity forged outside the kitchen and the ability to pay for the increasingly costly trappings of American prosperity. Now as many women work as those who stay home, single moms number in the millions, and the idea of "family" has evolved into countless permutations. But though women's lib saw speeches, sit-ins, and bra-burnings, burning dinner wasn't an option. The fairer sex still invariably found herself in the kitchen at mealtime, pressed upon to produce something tasty, quick, and easy. The food industry has kept up, continuing to target females by offering a panoply of products to help ease the burden of the typically overextended American life. Technology continues to march forward as well. Microwave and convection ovens, cellular phones, and the internet now allow us to order our groceries with the click of a finger, find a recipe in the blink of an eye, heat up our concoctions faster than ever, and invite friends and family to join us on a moment's notice.

But as with all great American trends, a counterculture thrived to provide an alternative to the convenience food camp. Since the 1950s, when James Beard scoffed at the Bisquick-and-Betty Crocker set, to the 1960s, when Julia Child first countered the convenience-food craze with her groundbreaking *The French Chef Cookbook*, food has taken divergent paths. Americans simultaneously embrace convenience foods—to the tune of tens of billions of dollars a year while looking for ways to get back to basics. This has resulted in an ever-greater selection in the frozen, canned, and packaged aisles and the proliferation of artisanal, organic, seasonal, and home-centric cuisine. Still, the majority of Americans are